HOW TO FIND TIME FOR
BETTER PREACHING
AND BETTER PASTORING

Books by Joseph E. McCabe
Published by The Westminster Press

*How to Find Time for Better Preaching
and Better Pastoring*

*Your First Year at College:
Letters to a College Freshman*

The Power of God in a Parish Program

HOW TO FIND TIME FOR

BETTER PREACHING

AND

BETTER PASTORING

by JOSEPH E. McCABE

THE WESTMINSTER PRESS • PHILADELPHIA

PUBLISHED BY THE WESTMINSTER PRESS ®
PHILADELPHIA, PENNSYLVANIA

PRINTED IN THE UNITED STATES OF AMERICA

Library of Congress Cataloging in Publication Data

McCabe, Joseph E., 1912–
  How to find time for better preaching and better
pastoring.

  1. Pastoral Theology.   2. Preaching.   I. Title.
BV4011.M23   253   73–10264
ISBN 0–664–20983–1

CONTENTS

PREFACE

"It pleased God by the foolishness of preaching to save them that believe." Those words of Paul, in the King James Version, prompted me to leave graduate school and enter theological seminary. They sustained me throughout my pastoral ministry.

"If Protestantism dies, the sword in its heart will be the sermon." Those words have haunted me from the time I heard them in my first pastorate a quarter of a century ago.

I believe both of the above statements about preaching to be absolutely true. The demands of the modern parish have caused a decline in the fine art of preaching. The endeavor of this book is to show how the pastor can greatly improve both his preaching and his pastoring, without any additional demands on his time.

JOSEPH E. McCABE

Coe College
Cedar Rapids, Iowa

1

THE DECLINE OF
THE PASTORAL ROLE

The decline of the pastoral role is one of the most obvious changes in the Protestant church in recent years.
A generation ago there still persisted the view that the
ordained man was to take the initiative in meeting his
parishioners between Sundays. Almost everyone over fifty
can remember the home call by the pastor. Rural America is replete with stories about the opening of the parlor
on two occasions: when there was a death in the family
and when the pastor came calling.

The idea that the pastor should get into every home
once a year was very much the expectation of the average congregation. Family-by-family visitation was simply
assumed to be a part of the normal pattern of ministry;
whether anything significant happened in the course of
the home call was a question seldom if ever raised. Most
pastors read a passage from the Bible and offered prayer
on these occasions. Undoubtedly some good resulted
from this type of pastoral relationship. No assessment is
intended here. The whole point is simply to observe that

what was once the normal expectation of every congregation, and a large part of the pastor's work schedule, has
significantly declined, where it has not completely disap-
peared.

The first reason for the decline in pastoral calling—that
part of the pastoral task with which we are most concerned here—is simply that so many additional demands
were made on the pastor. The growing emphasis on religious education called for large blocks of time, for the
pastor had to know the curriculum and had to adminis-
ter the program. A former generation never even heard
of Alcoholics Anonymous, of the God and Country
Award of the Boy Scouts, or of men's groups. The pastor's
new civic involvements ran the gamut from the P.T.A. to
community action groups. Then the very promising emphasis on small groups emerged. In addition to all this,
the pastor's counseling load grew apace. All these new
demands greatly reduced that portion of his time which
had previously been devoted to pastoral calling.

A second reason for the decline is to be found in the
changes that took place in the theological seminaries.
There was a time when the institutions that prepared
men for the ministry had the requirement that faculty
members must have had parish experience. Since over 90
percent of seminarians had that vocational goal in mind,
this requirement ensured a faculty well acquainted with
their students' future task. Then with the growth of specialization in the respective disciplines, that requirement
was gradually eliminated, as indeed it should have been.
Many changes that are necessary carry away some positive good. The requirement should have been dropped,
but one result was the lessening of emphasis on the pastoral role.

A further seminary development was that the curriculum, which by now had become greatly diversified and was being taught by scholarly specialists, placed less emphasis on practical theology. Following the lead of the church, or providing that lead, the seminary developed an atmosphere infused with social activism. Harsher critics claimed that sociology had replaced theology. Regardless of where the weight of the argument falls, it is clear that the parish, as a vocational choice, was falling far behind the total number of other options open to seminary graduates. Those who did choose the parish found themselves ill-prepared, or underprepared, for the task of developing and sustaining meaningful pastoral relationships. The decline of the pastoral role, especially as it involved calling, was inevitable.

The third, and by far the most decisive, reason for the decline in pastoral calling was the changed image that the pastor had of himself, of his life and work. He had heard of that older view of the cleric who came to tea at four in the afternoon, and he had the robust good sense to say that that was not for him. Likewise he had probably known the pastor who simply started out every afternoon to ring the doorbells of unsuspecting parishioners. Bridge parties were interrupted, no men were to be seen, and schoolchildren coming in and eager to dash off to play were held captive for the pastor's visit, which was about as inauspicious a beginning with the younger set as could be imagined.

Calling was often very poorly done, even by the ablest men, for they lacked definite objectives other than to let their people know they were in town. The concept of pastoral calling that will be urged in this book was presented to the dean of a distinguished theological seminary. After reading it, he wrote: "Your approach to pastoral calling reminds me how much wasted time and motion I used to mistake for that part of parish work."

Given the folk stories about the pastor's visit, and with such experiences as the above clearly in mind, a sizable number of the contemporary clergy rightly decided that this would not be their style. That was an honest and commendable decision. Seeing these counterfeits of the true pastoral relationship, they abandoned calling altogether. What they should have done was to throw out the dirty bath water and keep the baby.

At this point it may be instructive to take a brief look at the churches from which many of ours in America have sprung. In England and Scotland, as well as on a large part of the Continent, church attendance is at an all-time low. In the past hundred years the prophetic voice of the church has never been so irrelevant to social issues as it is today. But before that situation came into existence, another change could readily be observed. A deep gulf developed between the pastor and his congregation. The old, and often inept, pastoral calling declined. The view developed that the pastor was available, and that if the people wanted him, they knew where they could find him.

This aloofness of the clergy was brought home to me when I preached in Great Britain one Sunday. After the service I went to the door to greet the people. An elder sharply rebuked me, saying: "You should have gone to the retiring room; then if anyone wanted to see you, he could have looked you up."

In recent years American Protestantism has seen hundreds of pastors either leave the ministry altogether or stay on in bitter frustration of spirit. Many of them had expected their solid and correct Biblical expositions to galvanize their congregations into social action. When they encountered apathy, or outright opposition, their ministry turned sour. In some cases good men rightfully turned away from such churches. But in many cases the pastor was for the first time in his life right up against the harsh realities of human nature. If the Biblical doctrine of original sin had been near the surface of his consciousness, he would not have been so surprised. If he had realized that the gospel is needed precisely because people are as they are, and if he had gone to work with faithful pastoral relations, family by family, he might have been equally surprised at the result.

Disillusion and embitterment marked a significant number of men who graduated from theological seminary in the sixties. The social activism atmosphere of their seminary days, much as that emphasis was needed, ill-prepared them to deal with the recalcitrance of human nature as they were to encounter it in the parish. The bloom faded early from their ministries. The president of one of the largest seminaries in the Midwest pointed out this expectation among his students. "They want to go out and give people the word," he observed. The result could only be bitterness of soul and frustration of spirit.

It falls to my lot to visit with many pastors during the course of a year. At the most difficult time of the social action summons to the churches in the late sixties, I talked with some men who were utterly beaten and with others who still found a positive exhilaration in their work. Almost without exception the man for whom the glow had departed from his work had followed no careful program for establishing and maintaining the pastoral relationship. Likewise, in most cases where the church was alive and vital and the preacher in some measure felt that his work was not in vain, he was a man whose people felt his warmth and knew him as a faithful pastor.

My experience in this matter was recently corroborated by a church executive who has primary responsibility for working with churches where the congregation and the pastor are at odds. He wanted to be far more certain than I have indicated above that there was a very positive and direct correlation between pastoral care and the relationship between congregation and incumbent. He said he did not know a single situation where a man had been quite diligent about the pastoral function and still was, as he put it, "in trouble with his congregation." Conversely, he was quite emphatic that where there was a good relationship and a vital congregational life, there could be found a pastor who was diligent in the pastoral office, with a large amount of his time devoted to home visitation.

Can the pastoral role be significantly enhanced, or is it doomed to receive only those fractions of a man's time which unexpectedly come free amid the multitude of demands made upon him? Surely the need for pastoral care has never been greater. The secular is still driving out the sense of the sacred. The successful were never so harried. More marriages are more tenuous. The poor have a greater sense of helplessness. For many, longer life simply means longer time to worry. And every profession is in tension. The law is no longer that stable, firmly-set calling. The educator's landscape is a chaos of conflicting claims. The honest doctor knows that he knows less about the total body of medical knowledge than he would like to know. Public officials, from the city council or the sheriff to the Senate, are under fire. It is all too obvious to be labored further.

Right here it is essential for us to grasp the crucial role of the pastor. If a few years ago it seemed that he was becoming odd man out, now he is being seen again in many quarters as "the professional of whom all other professions stand most in need." President Nathan Pusey, of Harvard University, said that at the dedication of the Robert E. Speer Library at Princeton Theological Seminary. Here is the full passage:

> Many circumstances of our lives suggest that the informed, compassionate, understanding scholar-minister is the professional of whom all other professions stand most in need, for it is his function to speak to them of that kind of redemption or rededication which alone can give acceptable meaning to their efforts, and which is in the gospel's power, helped by a truly learned minister, widely to mediate.

The ordained man who disdains the traditional pastoral role may be overlooking one of the most decisive facts of life. The beginning place is to recognize that *every contact is a pastoral contact*. This is simply to say that whenever and under whatever circumstances there is a meeting of pastor and parishioner, something definitely takes place. Within the parishioner there are developing deep-seated and quite unconscious attitudes toward the pastor. Either the parishioner is "moving toward him, or moving away from him." Either the feeling is growing that the pastor is one to whom he could go with his deepest problems, or, on the negative side, the feeling is deepening that here is a man he would not really be open to, even when he needed a pastor most.

This positive or negative conditioning of the parishioner goes forward when he meets the pastor at the movies, on the golf course, at the P.T.A. meeting, or in the super-market.

Some pastors resent this basic fact of human nature. They want to be regarded "first of all as a man who has chosen the church as his vocation." That is all right; let him choose to be so regarded. The fact of life is that *every contact is a pastoral contact,* with the above move-ment of personality definitely taking place. If a man resents this too much, he should reexamine his motives for seeking ordination. Perhaps what he was really seek-ing was an opportunity to tell people what they ought to do. That is his prophetic role, though it is really the Scrip-tures speaking through him that do the telling. But the prophetic is always being conditioned by the pastoral. To forget that, or to resist it overmuch, is simply to be working against a basic fact of human nature and to be undermining one's effectiveness.

Pastoral calling takes time, much time. Just how some precious hours might be allocated during the week, and even how additional time can be freed for the task, will be the main concern of the later chapters of this book. The point to be made here is that pastoral calling can be very effective. The following is taken from the review of a book about the parish that appeared in one of the most influential religious publications:

"Different members of the family can be engaged in significant dialogue if the pastor will just take the trouble to arrange to call by appointment and be sure that all members of the family will be present. The pastoral call [is] an opportunity to initiate and continue dialogue on a significant level involving each member of the family.

For instance, questions can be raised concerning the nature and mission of the church, such as: Are you satisfied with the program of our congregation? What do you think that our church should be doing? What do you see as the purpose of the church?

"Such questions may very well motivate, at least the older members of the family, to do some serious reading in this area—perhaps to enroll in one of the study groups of the church to continue this dialogue that the pastor has introduced at deeper levels. Dialogue initiated in pastoral calling can be continued through the Sunday morning message as some of the subjects of pastoral conversation during the week are integrated into the sermon. At other times, issues raised in the sermon could be the subject of the dialogue of pastoral conversation in the following week. Pastoral calling does not need to be the "chit-chat" that it so frequently is." (*Church Management,* December, 1968.)

I recently attended a church which I do not usually get to on a Sunday morning. At the time for the announcements the preacher said: "If I can be helpful to anyone, don't hesitate to phone me. I can come to your home almost any evening of the week at nine o'clock." The man has a reputation for diligently visiting his people. The church was well filled the Sunday I was there, and the budget is oversubscribed.

Reuel Howe has been in the forefront of efforts to renew the church. He sees relationships as the clue to the vitality of the fellowship. He writes: "Dialogue is to love, what blood is to the body. When the flow of blood stops, the body dies. When dialogue stops, love dies and resentment and hate are born. But dialogue can restore a dead relationship. Indeed, this is the miracle of dialogue;

it can bring relationship into being, and it can bring into being a relationship that has died." (*The Miracle of Dialogue,* p. 3; The Seabury Press, 1963.)

Every pastor has a long list of people whose names are on the parish roll but who are far from the center of the church's life. Every study demonstrates that the lapsed can be restored more readily than new people can be won. The pastor should ponder Howe's words: "Dialogue . . . can bring into being a relationship that has died." And then he should honestly ask what opportunities for dialogue he is providing to those who are out at the edges.

Does all this sound like a retreat from that prophetic stance which now marks large segments of the American church? Just the opposite is intended. That prophetic emphasis was long overdue. It constitutes one of the most hopeful signs of the times. Far from deprecating it, we would stress the point that the enhancement of the pastoral role, and especially effective calling, is intended to meet human needs. Now we turn to a consideration of how pastoral care, and especially calling, is related to the prophetic task of the pastor and the church.

2

THE PASTORAL

PRECEDES THE PROPHETIC

The most decisive movement in the churches of America in this century may well be their recall to a prophetic ministry. The prevailing culture had begun to dominate the church. Unless it was the thrust for Christian unity, nothing is comparable to the summons to the church to take up again its ancient prophetic task. Immediately following World War II, church membership and the role of organized religion grew at a pace which should have warned us that here was something less than the real thing. Biblical religion and the demands for discipleship held forth by the New Testament are not likely to receive such easy acceptance. The necessary corrective set in during the sixties. The prophetic task of the church was accepted. Organized religion became deeply involved in the struggle for peace and justice.

And with what result? Both peace and justice were advanced. But the other side of the story is something else. Membership in the standard-brand churches is in decline. Attendance at worship services is lower than it has been for decades. Stewardship, as expressed in terms of dollars, bears no identifiable relationship to the material prosperity of church members. Alienation from the church is widespread. Frustration and cynicism have come to characterize many pastors. The whole story is too sad and too familiar to be rehearsed in further detail.

The call to the prophetic was absolutely necessary if the church was to save its own soul. Preparation for the task could scarcely have been more inept. Precisely when the pastoral relationship should have been at its finest in order for people to receive the prophetic witness, that relationship, as we have seen, was at an all-time low. The prophet will always have a hard time of it. He can accept that fact on the warrant of Scripture and of history. The difficulty was compounded by the prophet's having largely abandoned his pastoral task, the other half of the ministry to which he had been called and ordained.

Recent political life and church life have both revealed the deep-seated prejudices in our country. The average American by and large just doesn't like people of a color other than his own. Most Americans aren't enthusiastic about the United Nations. They respond very favorably to talk about cutting back foreign aid. There is prejudice in many quarters against the poor. The concept of a worldwide fellowship of Christians is embraced, until it is pointed out that millions of our Christian brothers and sisters go to bed hungry every night. And we are light-years from a Biblical standard of stewardship. Main-line Protestants do not give 2 percent of their annual income to the church, for combined local and worldwide mission. Giving less than one fiftieth of our income is not likely to merit, "Well done, thou good and faithful servant." Both the Old and the New Testament deal forthrightly with the matter of money and how its use is a reflection of the faith of the owner. It will take the prophetic, embodied in a pastor, to drain off those prejudices and enable people to establish priorities with some semblance of Christian commitment.

Of course such a cataloging of national and church shortcomings only underscores the need for the gospel. If human nature were already perfect, there would have been no need for the incarnation. Our daily crucifixions of the good make the judgment of God imperative, in order that we may repent and accept our tasks in furthering the Kingdom. But "cheap grace," to use Bonhoeffer's phrase, only insulates people from that radical commitment which is at the heart of Christian discipleship. Many of our clergy were unwilling to palm off cheap grace, and that was to their credit. But they were also unwilling to earn their prophetic standing with their people by being faithful and diligent pastors, in which case they were lazy, or unimaginative. Perhaps they didn't really like people at all, just humanity.

Confidence that we could deal with these stubborn social problems, which was so bright a promise in the sixties, is waning. Many secular social activists, who started out with the noblest of intentions to better the world, are disillusioned. Why? They have run smack up against the stubborn facts of human nature, and they had no Biblical doctrine of man for guidance. The third chapter of Genesis is relevant to man's plight. When social activists run out into the desert of despair because of their experience with life as it really is, then the Christian goes right on affirming that social structures must be changed, and so must the human heart. But that is a prophetic stance. It is the antidote to disillusion, and succor to those who all along have understood the magnitude of the human problem.

The man who takes seriously his ordination vows to be a prophet should also take seriously the Biblical material which points the way to effectiveness. He should also know particular case histories in the recent American church where the prophetic ministry got results. Let us consider some examples of both.

How many preachers have held forth on these words from the book of Ezekiel: "Son of man, I have made thee a watchman unto the house of Israel: therefore hear the word at my mouth, and give them warning from me." There follow the dire warnings of the consequences of failure to heed the prophet. But the preacher should also take very seriously the two verses which immediately precede that commission: "Then I came to them of the captivity at Tel-abib, that dwelt by the river of Chebar, and I sat where they sat."

There is the guidance for the modern prophet as he contemplates the word he is to deliver from the pulpit: "I sat where they sat." It is precisely this solidarity with his people which is precedent to the effectual utterance of the prophetic word.

It is doubtful if anyone other than Martin Luther King has exercised such an effective prophetic ministry in America as Ernest Fremont Tittle. Reinhold Niebuhr wrote of him: "I can only say that for many years I have constantly held up Dr. Tittle as an example of the kind of integrity and courage which saves the church from futility." (*The Christian Century*, Feb. 7, 1973, p. 179.) For many years he was the preacher to a silk-stocking congregation in Evanston. When Tittle went into the pulpit on Sunday morning, he knew that much of the economic and political power structure of Chicago and the State of Illinois was before him. He never wavered from his clear call for racial and economic justice. It was strong medicine. A leading Chicago industrialist was once asked how he could listen to such preaching Sunday after Sunday. His reply was related to me as follows:

"When my wife died in the hospital, all the world went black. I just started out, walking aimlessly, and found myself along Lake Michigan. Hour after hour I walked, my darkness as thick as the night. Every time I looked back, there was Tittle, just a little way behind me, following like the hound of heaven. I walked all night, and all night he followed. Finally, when dawn was breaking over the lake, Tittle came up, took my arm, and said: 'Let's go get some breakfast.' I'll listen to that man anytime."

In the New Testament we have those striking passages of Paul calling down the judgment of God upon certain practices in the church. "I am astonished that you are so quickly deserting him who called you in the grace of Christ and turning to a different gospel. . . . As we have said before, so now I say again, If any one is preaching to you a gospel contrary to that which you received, let him be accursed. . . . Am I now seeking the favor of men, or of God? Or am I trying to please men? . . . O foolish Galatians! Who has bewitched you, before whose eyes Jesus Christ was publicly portrayed as crucified? . . . Are you so foolish? . . . Did you experience so many things in vain? . . . How can you turn back again to the weak and beggarly elemental spirits, whose slaves you want to be once more?"

Now that is strong stuff for any congregation to hear

from a preacher. What man would not like to be able to be so blunt and so direct. And why was it effective? Was it because he had impeccable credentials? Here they are: "Paul an apostle—not from men nor through man, but through Jesus Christ and God the Father." Even that call and ordination—as though he were a modern Phi Beta Kappa and graduate of the denomination's leading seminary—would not have given him power to preach such a powerful word. The secret is right there in the same message, where Paul says: "I bear you witness that, if possible, you would have plucked out your eyes and given them to me." The decisive relationship had been established long before, and out of that solidarity he could speak with prophetic authority.

A church in Philadelphia did the following things, all within the space of three years. They adopted the requirement that all prospective members should attend a series of membership seminars conducted by the pastor on Sunday evenings. They made premarriage counseling mandatory for all who were to be married in that sanctuary. They required parents of children that were to be baptized to attend a seminar on the meaning of Christian baptism. They heard the preacher say many times from the pulpit that to whom much is given, of him shall much be required. And they increased their giving to benevolences 300 percent in three years.

Does anyone think a man can come to town, announce such an agenda for the church, and get it adopted? The pastor did announce on his arrival that he planned to visit every home in the parish, in the evening, and by appointment. And though it took him nearly two years to get around to every home, the word got around before him. There was always some dialogue elicited about the meaning of Christian discipleship and church membership, always an inquiry about expectations from the church, and always Scripture-reading and prayer. When the above agenda was presented, item by item, discreetly spaced, there was enthusiastic acceptance. But the "price" for the proposals had been paid in pastoral faithfulness. (I have described fully this program in *The Power of God in a Parish Program.*)

Here is something that goes to the heart of the problem: "Often ministers moving to new parishes will import to the new situation the same program that they used in their former pastorate. And they scratch their head, wondering why the people are not more responsive and more responsible. A church program must be formulated out of the give-and-take of a dialogical relationship of pastor and people. In such a relationship God can speak a living word that is active to create community. God speaks through the minister to the people, but God also speaks through the people to him. This is the very nature of the dialogue of the community of faith." (*Church Management,* December, 1968.)

The letter to the Romans stands as Paul's most definitive work. The vitality of the church can be measured in successive ages by the prominence given this document, all the way from Augustine to Karl Barth. If prophecy is a "showing forth of the mind and will of God," then Romans is nowhere surpassed in all the Scriptures. But turn to the last chapter and you will see that it is no unknown newcomer who thus addresses people. His pastoral affection shows through:

"Greet Prisca and Aquila, my fellow workers in Christ. . . . Greet my beloved Epaenetus. . . . Greet Mary. . . . Greet Andronicus and Junias. . . . Greet Ampliatus, my beloved in the Lord. Greet Urbanus, our fellow worker in Christ, and my beloved Stachys. Greet Apelles, who is approved in Christ. . . . Greet those in the Lord who belong to the family of Narcissus." And the list continues: "Tryphaena and Tryphosa, Persis, Rufus, Asyncritus, Phlegon, Hermes, Patrobas, Hermas, Philologus, Julia, Nereus, and Olympas."

And when they were gathered together for worship in that primitive Christian community, and heard their names read off, they were doubly assured of "him who is able to strengthen you according to my gospel and the preaching of Jesus Christ." Every sight of those strange names should recall to us that great pastoral heart of Paul.

"The list of names, each with its appropriate greeting, gives us a faint conception of the close and affectionate relations which existed between Paul and his converts. We unconsciously assume that the apostle may have been a great man but that he was probably a forbidding companion. Having read through Romans, some of us might view with alarm the prospect of spending an informal evening in Paul's company. We may study his letters for the good of our souls, but we would not instinctively choose him as a friend. There is plenty of evidence, however, to prove that he not only felt deep affection for his converts, but aroused in them an answering regard." (*The Interpreter's Bible*, Vol. 9, pp. 658–659.)

I think I have heard all the reasons advanced why a pastor cannot spend two evenings a week on pastoral calling during the first year or two in a new parish. But men in new situations keep right on doing it. I recently talked with a man whose installation I attended in a neighboring church which has something like seven hundred members. During the service of installation we sang the hymn that meant so much to all of us in seminary days: "God of the prophets! Bless the prophets' sons; Elijah's mantle o'er Elisha cast." It is a noble and moving plea, and at ordination this is exactly what is done symbolically. The second stanza defines the prophets' task:

> Anoint them prophets! Make their ears attent
> To Thy divinest speech; their hearts awake
> To human need; their lips make eloquent
> To gird the right and every evil break.

At ordination this pastor was set apart by the authority of Christ and the church for his prophetic role. Now he has been installed as pastor of the congregation. He is the only full-time member of the staff. Those seven hundred members must represent some three hundred families. He plans to call in every home on the parish roll, in the evening, by appointment.

Two past moderators of what is now The United Presbyterian Church U.S.A. come to mind when I think of the pastoral and the prophetic. Eugene Smathers had all of his ministry in rural churches and small villages. His people loved him, and he got more done in the way of social action than dozens of men more favorably placed. Henry Sloane Coffin was the preacher at the Madison Avenue Presbyterian Church in New York City, then president of Union Seminary in that city, and moderator. As seminary president he once complained that it was difficult to get students out of the library and onto the picket line, whereas in another generation it was hard to get them off the picket line and into the library. He knew both emphases well.

But first of all he was a pastor. During his Madison Avenue days it was not uncommon for Coffin to call at the East Side apartment of a wealthy family, only to be greeted with the word that they were not members of his church. To which his reply was that he would appreciate an opportunity to visit with the maid, for it was she he had come to visit. Not long ago a middle-age pastor was talking of men in the ministry whom he admired. Referring to Coffin, he said: "Uncle Henry, now there was a man who believed in calling."

Read again Paul's letter to Philemon. It is a model of pastoral relationships. First of all, there are the greetings, by name: "To Philemon our beloved fellow worker and Apphia our sister and Archippus our fellow soldier, and the church in your house." Always there is that personal note. Then he spells it right out to Philemon, and forthrightly tells him what he wants him to do, something that is going to be very distasteful to Philemon:

"Though I am bold enough in Christ to command you to do what is required . . . ." Paul could lay it on the line. He was asking a master to take back a runaway slave, knowing that the master had the legal right to kill him. That's getting involved in social action. But Paul asks Philemon to "receive him as you would receive me."

Of course Onesimus had wronged his master, whether he had stolen from him or simply caused him the loss of all those man-hours of work by skipping town. So Paul writes: "If he has wronged you at all, or owes you anything, charge that to my account." It was the pastoral relationship that enabled Paul to write: "Confident of your obedience, I write to you, knowing that you will do even more than I say." It is the constant miracle that parishioners will do things that go against the grain simply be-

cause a concerned pastor whom they love has laid out the
course of Christian duty.

Of course the pastoral role takes time, much time.
When a man contemplates calling in every home at the
outset of his ministry in a particular church, he has set
for himself a formidable task. There are strenuous ob-
jections. There is the time needed for one's own family,
the meetings to be attended, the necessary personal recreation, the evening reading schedule—and all the rest.
But men keep right on doing it. Consider the following
excerpts from a letter I received after writing on the
subject in some detail:

"I have been calling upon every home of my parish all
year and since that is some six hundred calls, you can
well imagine how busy I have been. I spend about an
hour in each home and am taking all the time necessary
to do it on that basis, finding it very useful in my first
year in the parish. I can't tell you how valuable this
whole program has been in cementing and establishing a
real relationship to my people and in the future development of our own program here in _____. I also
used your thought of a pamphlet to people about the
occasions in which the minister might be of service to
his congregation except that, of course, I abridged your
general program into my own thoughts and into my
own program here. That also has proved to be an ex-
tremely valuable idea. All in all, it was the soundest
possible kind of guidance for a man beginning a new
parish and one in which he expects to remain for a con-
siderable period of time and hopes to make a significant
contribution."

Not many contemporary preachers in Scotland, and
even fewer in America, have read Richard Baxter's *The*

Reformed Pastor, and not many on that side of the Atlantic can fill a church. The language is quaint, but the call for the lifting up of the pastoral office is clear and strong. James Stewart of Edinburgh, when referring to Baxter's book, advised his students: "Sell your bed and buy it." When Stewart preached at Morningside, the church was always filled. The people knew that the prophet loved them.

From a very small town in Illinois a man in his first year out of theological seminary writes: "I have a terrific need for effective pastoral calling. Your material on twelve times to call a minister has hit me, and, I am sure, my congregation, right between the eyes." That man is no metropolitan divine, but he is on his way to a pastoral relationship that will enhance his prophetic task.

There is just one more New Testament passage to which I would call attention. Each pastor will decide for himself how relevant it is for his ministry. "The sheep hear his voice, and he calls his own sheep by name and leads them out. When he has brought out all his own, he goes before them, and the sheep follow him, for they know his voice. A stranger they will not follow, but they will flee from him, for they do not know the voice of strangers."

Jesus had a good many things to say to Peter before he changed that blustering bravado into a man he could use for the Kingdom. It is not without significance that the last recorded words of Jesus to Peter were: "Feed my sheep."

Management principles do not determine the pastor's task. That is set by human nature and the Biblical resources. But adherence to sound management principles can greatly enhance his work and further the Kingdom.

Any sound management analysis of the pastor's task today would show that he simply has too many assignments. The variety of expectations is just too great for
any man to accomplish them all with a fair degree of
satisfaction, either to himself or to those involved with
him. On this matter of the multiplicity of assignments,
little relief is in sight for the single-pastor church.

A sound management analysis would show further that
the pastor's communications are emotionally blocked.
Our people do not like the prophetic. They do not really
hear it in the depths of their being. Time with his people
is the most effective way for the pastor to work at this
problem. It is essential for him to be with them if they
are really to hear and to accept his prophetic ministry.
His time to be with people has been greatly curtailed by
the multiplicity of his assignments, and this lessening of
time with the parishioners prevents effective communica-
tion of his message. Significant help with the latter problem is available, as we shall see later.

There is only one situation worse than the neglect of
the pastoral office which blocks the prophetic. That is the
deliberate and calculated false use of the pastoral role
to develop a personality cult, with never the disturbing
prophetic note. It is the blight of the Protestant ministry
that congregations will hold their idol in almost total
reverence if he will cater to their prejudices and keep
silent on the big issues of the times. The prophet who
neglects the pastoral office will be ineffective, but the
popular pastor who avoids the prophetic is the modern
betrayer of the gospel.

We have all known Protestants who are most laudatory
of their pastor, praising him to the skies on every social
occasion, but who have never had the white light of the

gospel cast on their sins. Their church may be a fine social club, but they have never heard of the call of God to become involved in the death struggles of our culture. Neglect is better than betrayal. But the pastoral neglect that renders the prophetic ineffectual is not necessary. The later chapters of this book will suggest the way to strengthen both the pastoral office and the prophetic preaching.

If there is one truth for our time that should be placarded over every pastor's study desk, it is this: *The pastoral precedes the prophetic.* The question that should be asked of every seminarian before he opts for the parish ministry is this: Are you committed to that full ministry to which you feel called, the pastoral as well as the prophetic? Scripture and history document the truth, now so painfully obvious to many pastors whose prophetic role was not accepted by their congregations—the pastor earns his right to be a prophet by the faithful fulfillment of the pastoral office.

The prophetic without the pastoral is ineffective.

The pastoral without the prophetic is a betrayal.

The pastoral with the prophetic is the Biblical calling.

Faithfulness to the Biblical calling will free a man from the twin impostors of success or failure.

3

RESOURCES FOR
THE PASTORAL PROGRAM

It is not my intention here to develop a complete compendium of resources for the pastoral task, but rather to outline the main points for an effective home-visitation program. Each pastor will develop both his skills and the material he finds most helpful as he goes along in the work. What is offered here is a framework with which to make a meaningful beginning.

1. *The Stewardship of Time*

The modern pastor may very well raise the objection that the pressure of events simply prevents his having time for pastoral calling. It is true, as has been emphasized here several times, that today's pastor has demands on him which a previous generation never knew. However, the greatest need is not for the reduction of the expectations but for a stringent discipline in the use of time presently available. The pastor is free to develop his own work schedule. By and large he is not accountable to anyone as to how he arranges his workday or his workweek. As a consequence, there is often a laxity in this area which is simply appalling. The pastor is rightly unhappy when a layman with leadership talents will not spend an hour or two a week in the service of the church. But who passes judgment on the pastor who fritters away half a dozen hours during the week when he could be working most effectively? Is the ordained pastor, who has been set over a congregation for their spiritual welfare, to be less disciplined than the high school basketball coach or the insurance salesman?

Discipline produces freedom. Careful and strict stewardship of working hours enables a man to have much free time with his family and planned recreation, which is necessary to both physical and mental health. Time is the pastor's most precious resource. Careful scheduling of the time available produces freedom. How to release more time for the pastoral office and how also to improve the preaching from the pulpit will be the main concerns of the following chapters of this book.

Suppose a pastor definitely plans to be out calling two evenings a week, from seven o'clock until nine thirty. In that time he can have three very meaningful visits in the homes of his people. Assume that there will be twelve weeks a year when this schedule cannot be kept. It is necessary to allow for vacations, conflicts, and weeks such as Christmas and Holy Week when it just should not be attempted. This still leaves the pastor with forty weeks a year. If he makes six calls a week, there will be a total of two hundred and forty home visits a year. That calling schedule would get him into each home of a five-hundred-member parish every year and into each home of a thousand-member parish every other year.

If he were to adopt only half the above schedule, he could be in each home of the five-hundred-member parish every other year and in the thousand-member parish every three or four years. That lesser calling schedule would be pure gain over the situation as it exists today in hundreds of parishes. Of course I am talking about meaningful pastoral visitation, not the random afternoon doorbell pushing that is so artificial and so ineffective.

Occasionally I meet a pastor who tries very hard to limit his workday to the hours between eight and five. I have never known a vital parish where anything like that was possible. Of course evenings with his family, and other times together with them, should be as carefully scheduled as calling and other church work. But one who objects to evening work in the parish should look at the schedule of my middle-age friend who sells life insurance.

I am writing this at nine thirty in the evening. A few minutes ago I phoned that insurance salesman's home. His wife said he was out working. Now I have just reached him. He has been working all evening and is just finishing a report. He tells me that some weeks he works only one or two evenings, but then when things are busy he works as many as five or six evenings. Three, he says, is probably the average.

Within days of writing this I visited with a graduate who has been out of the college about a dozen years. (If he had gone to theological seminary, he would now be ready for his second parish.) He sells stocks and bonds. I jotted down what he said as he told me of his work. "First you classify that long list of names. [We will discuss classifying in a moment.] After that it's just hard work. You must establish a good rapport before you can discuss any specific plan. You get their confidence in you before you can urge any specific investment. Of course, there's evening work—that's the only time some people are available." Of course, these fellows are selling a service and a product in which they believe and to which they have devoted themselves, namely, insurance, stocks, and bonds.

2. *Classifying the Calls*

If a pastor looks at the parish roll with six hundred names on it, he may be daunted by the number of evenings he thinks would be required to make all the calls. But let him analyze that church roll. It probably represents fewer than three hundred family units. The list of shut-ins will reduce the number of evening calls, for the most effective time to visit these people is late morning or afternoon. The number of widows and widowers will further reduce the list. Many of them can also be marked for afternoon calls. Likewise, afternoon visits can be arranged with the retired couples.

The obvious point is that the evening hours are so precious that they should be reserved for those situations where it would not be possible to see all the members of a family at any other time. A church roll of six hundred will probably have around two hundred and twenty-five families for whom the evening call is the most effective. The others can be marked for the more readily available daylight hours. If the pastor makes three home calls two evenings a week for forty weeks, he will get into every home within a year. That prospect should be deeply pleasing, whereas at first sight of the parish roll, the pastor may have felt the assignment to be overwhelming.

Classification of the calls is just good stewardship of those evening hours. It transforms a long list of names into a manageable program.

3. *A Sense of the Prophetic*

The pastor must have an antidote for the pallid and ineffective calling mentioned in Chapter 1. Perhaps the very best way for him to prepare for the work is to remember that he is just as much a prophet when calling as he is when in his study or in the pulpit. Do not think that pastoral calling is simply fulfilling the priestly function. It is a vast misunderstanding of the situation to think you are to bring the "consolations of religion" to a parishioner who has consistently absented himself from worship services or who is disaffected by the church's social involvement. Perhaps the most effective ministry you can have with such a parishioner is just to bring out the New Testament, and as you turn the pages, let your remarks be something like this:

"Here Jesus said: 'I have come not to bring peace, but a sword.'"

"Again he said: 'It would be better for him to have a great millstone fastened round his neck and to be drowned in the depth of the sea.'"

"Here Jesus is speaking to some very respectable religious people, and he says: 'Woe to you, . . . hypocrites! . . . You serpents, you brood of vipers, how are you to escape being sentenced to hell?'"

"Here is what he said to the people in his hometown, concerning his life's work: 'The Spirit of the Lord is upon me, because he has anointed me to preach good news to the poor. He has sent me to proclaim release to the captives and recovering of sight to the blind, to set at liberty those who are oppressed, to proclaim the acceptable year of the Lord.' "

If the man has a quarrel, let it be with the Lord.

If you have asked for the appointment, the assumption is that you have something to say. Sometimes the pastor must be courageous enough to be prophetic when he is face-to-face with an individual or a couple, not just when he is in the relatively comfortable situation of preaching to a congregation. One thing is certain: if the above passages are referred to by a faithful and sincere pastor, the one who hears the reading will never forget the pastor's visit. Hearing the words might give the one visited a bad night, but that, of course, could be the beginning of a better day. Do not hesitate to fulfill your prophetic calling in the pastoral situation. There is as great a need for the prophetic in visitation as there is in preaching—both being by the concerned pastor who knows his people not only in the church but in their homes.

4. *The Content of the Dialogue*

When a committed layman lives with the problems of wages and prices, materials and budgets, with abrasive personnel above him or below him in the organization, he doesn't want the pastor to be a hail-fellow-well-met, as though the pastor was simply one of his more congenial associates at the office. It takes a pastoral heart to be able to say quite honestly to such a man: "How are things with you, spiritually?" That is the exact manner in which John Sutherland Bonnell at Fifth Avenue Presbyterian Church in New York City often phrased the question to a parishioner. Immediately the conversation was raised above either the Dow Jones average for the day or an exchange of golf handicaps.

Here is a pastor who objects to that Bonnell question, and could not possibly use it. I am reminded of a social gathering of a group of pastors where the discussion came around to Billy Graham and evangelism. Most of us were pastors in main-line churches where the fervor for evangelism was not quite at fever pitch. Some were objecting to the whole idea of mass evangelism. An older man with most of his lifetime in the ministry quietly said: "I like the way Billy does it, better than the way we're not doing it."

Each pastor must develop his own terminology for eliciting dialogue on a meaningful level, if there is to be something more than small talk, which is so essential at the outset but can be so damning if it characterizes the entire visit. True, not every man can use Bonnell's expression to good effect. But it is far better to risk stumbling with words like that than to fritter away the time with no decisive encounter at all. Develop your own method for moving the conversation toward something significant.

This means that you must be alert as the time goes along and decide in what direction you want the conversation to move. The dialogue with faithful members of the church should be quite different from that with someone who has been estranged by a social pronouncement of the denomination. The visit with a young couple who are just establishing a home bears little resemblance to the call on an aged person. A call where the pastor knows there is little enthusiasm for the church is vastly different from a call in the home of the church school superintendent. The discerning pastor will understand that there are as many differences in the homes in which he calls as there are differences between the people who come to his study for counseling. In the latter situation his training has alerted him to the wide variety of personal problems, and he would never dream of treating them all alike. Just so, it is the unimaginative sameness of some home calls that can be so deadly to the pastor's spirit and so ineffective.

The pastor should develop conversational materials which, through experience, he finds to be effective. For instance, one does not get far in visitation these days without encountering people hostile toward the local church for some community involvement or toward the denomination for some social pronouncement. Now, the great majority of these are people for whom Dwight D. Eisenhower remains a national hero, and from my point of view rightly so. When visiting these people the pastor can have in reserve, among other things, a quotation from Eisenhower. It is effective to remind them quietly of what Eisenhower said to the meeting of the World Council of Churches at Evanston:

We hope that you will touch our imagination, remind us again and again of the vision without which the people perish. Give us criticism in the light of religious ideals. Kindle anew in us a desire to strive for moral greatness and to show us where we fall short. We shall listen if you speak to us as the prophet spoke in the days of old. (*The Christian Century*, Sept. 1, 1954, p. 1049.)

Some evening the pastor will come across the confident humanist, though his tribe is declining. He will be either a nominal member of the church or a member of a family in which someone holds membership in the church. It is to get at the likes of him that I always asked for an appointment on an evening when all members of the family could be present, not only those who were members of the church. The type is usually an intellectual, or one falsely so called. If you have had some real encounter, write him a letter next day. He probably thinks quite highly of T. S. Eliot. You could quote the lines from *The Rock* that begin, "Why should men love the Church?" and go on to speak of the way in which the church has met the needs of the people. We have all known cynics, especially in the academic world, to whose condition Eliot is speaking. Put those lines in your letter and it will not wind up in the humanist's wastebasket, at least not until he has read it twice.

Then there is the honest critic who knows all the shortcomings of the church. Admit them. Add a few he hadn't heard about. Then loosen him up with Bishop Warburton's commentary: "The Church, like the Ark of Noah, is worth saving; not for the sake of the unclean beasts and vermin that almost filled it, and probably made most noise and clamor in it, but for the little corner of rationality, that was as much distressed by the stink within, as by the tempest without." And say in a paraphrase that "if it weren't for the storm outside, I couldn't stand the smell inside." At times that's a true assessment, and it helps to say so quite frankly with the right kind of critic. Then invite him to come aboard.

We live in the day of the sports hero. The teen-ager who is passing up church should be reminded of the terrific pressures on top sports figures. Name one whom you know to be faithful to church, or name the university quarterback who gives leadership in the Christian athletes movement, or whoever is making the contemporary scene and making his Christian witness at the same time. A major-league baseball pitcher, a consistent twenty-game winner, lived near our last parish. He was a devoted churchman; his name came into many home calls, for he was the idol of the sports crowd. Recently I talked with five students who are giving up this entire year at college to travel around the country and witness to their faith. Don't be a name-dropper to young people, but do know the names they know, and who are committed.

Consider the atmosphere of two very different calls on the aged. In the first case there has been success, but very little lasting satisfaction. It is quite possible to be surfeited with success and still have an empty heart. And the emptiness comes through in the dialogue. Try quoting Ruskin: "O why did not one tell me that the colours would fade, and that the glory of the earth would vanish; and that the soul asks and must have . . . something more splendid than this earth can give it?" Ruskin said that after he had reached the pinnacle of art and art criticism, with an appointment to the Oxford faculty. His words, quietly spoken by the sincere pastor, may help a man to recognize his true state and to provide an opening for a discussion of the adequacy of Christ.

The second case is that of the old and lonely who fear death and for whom life is a burden. You want to come out with the assurance of the presence of Christ. Since for many older people today the vital years were those when Eisenhower was President, you could relate the following passage, which is adapted from *Crusade in*

Europe. American troops are moving up toward the Rhine River. Ike writes:

"We joined some of them and found the troops remarkably eager to finish the job. . . . Nevertheless, as we walked along I fell in with one young soldier who seemed silent and depressed. 'How are you feeling, son?' I asked. 'General,' he said, 'I'm awful nervous. I was wounded two months ago and just got back from the hospital yesterday. I don't feel so good.' 'Well,' I said to him, 'you and I are a good pair then, because I'm nervous, too. . . . Maybe if we just walk along together to the river, we'll be good for each other.' 'Oh,' he said, 'I meant I *was* nervous; I'm not anymore. I guess it's not so bad around here.' "

To relate that incident is the legitimate use of a folk hero incident to lead into a discussion of the presence of Christ. I cite it here because many have identified with that story and it gives the pastor the opening to say: "How much more strengthening is the companionship of Christ, who said: 'Lo, I am with you alway, even unto the end of the world.' "

There is a wealth of excellent resource material from the mission field that is available for good use in pastoral calling. Remind the faithful family that this very day they have fed a hungry family in India, or helped a clinic in the African bush, or maintained an Ethiopian boy on his scholarship for the week. It is all a million miles from their awareness, but when you remind them of such specifics, in their home with all its conflicting requests for spending, you are developing stewardship.

The pastor who is calling by appointment has an enormous initial advantage. He has asked for the visit with the entire family. He is taking his precious evening time to come to their house. The whole concept of the shared ministry of the church in which this family has a part can be clearly developed. What a loss if the visit is not much different from one with the wealthy man's broker or the union member's foreman.

The plea here is for the pastor to develop material for the content of the dialogue in the home. The above is simply intended to be illustrative. Don't preach this material, for then you have given it away to the entire congregation and it comes as stale stuff when you refer to it in your calls. Rather, use such material in individual homes only; then the bloom is always fresh.

5. *The Scripture-Reading*

There are multitudes of Christian homes in this country where Scripture has never been read. Don't hurl it at the heads of people, as though it were something magical to lend authenticity to your call. All that has gone before is intended to make the reading meaningful. Brevity and simplicity are the two guides. At a natural lull in the conversation, say something such as this: "It has been good to be in your home. I feel that we know each other much better. Before retiring tonight, I will pray for you, as I hope each of you will pray for me and for our church which Christ has given us to share. Now, before I go, let us think seriously together about this passage from the letter to the Ephesians."

The following are some appropriate Scripture passages for reading on the occasions designated:

For the first call in a new parish—Eph. 4:1-6, 11-13
During Advent—Isa. 9:2, 6-7

At Christmastide—I John 1:1–3
Near New Year's—I Chron. 29:10–15
During Lent—Isa. 53:3–6, 12b
At Eastertide—John 20:24–29
A reading in winter—Ps. 51:6–12
A reading in springtime—Matt. 13:3–9
A reading in summer—Ps. 121
A reading in the fall—Ps. 1
A reading for Thanksgiving season—Ps. 100
Personal responsibility for the Kingdom—Matt. 5:13–16
The Christian understanding of love—I Cor., ch. 13
Christ's gracious invitation—Matt. 11:28–29

6. *The Prayer*

Who can suggest for another person the content of the pastoral prayer? (Incidentally, the most appropriate place to speak of a "pastoral prayer" is in connection with the home visit rather than in the order of service on Sunday morning.) Like every call, every prayer varies. Only let it "fit" the situation and not have the smell of the study about it. Here are expressions incorporated into the prayer which people have said were helpful:

In any home: "May this home be an example of Christian living and sharing."

Where there is a married couple: "We ask you to renew and deepen the marriage vows of your servants."

Where someone is absent from the home, at college, or in military service: "While he is apart from us tonight, we thank you that he is not separated from you."

When there are children present: "We thank you for all who make life good for us; for children with whom we play; for teachers, who help us to know more about your world; and for the church, where we learn about Jesus."

Where there is illness at a distance, or when someone is in the hospital: "We pray for him who is dear to us and, we know, dear to you. Surround him with your light and love."

When a baby has been born or adopted: "With the coming of this child may we come closer to one another and closer to you."

When there has been a death: "We thank you, our Father, that neither life nor death can separate us from you, or, in the end, from one another."

Near a wedding anniversary: "We thank you for love and tender affection. We thank you even for the dark days we have known if they have brought us closer to one another and closer to you."

If the name of the former pastor has come into the conversation: "We thank you for the ministry of our friend, John Smith, and we ask your blessing upon him tonight."

In any home: "Help each of us to fulfill his ministry, whether as lay people or ordained."

If free prayer comes hard for you, use these expressions. Write some of your own. By writing them in your study, you will be better prepared to use them in prayer in homes without stumbling. But if you do stumble and some infelicitous wording comes out, don't be concerned. The pastoral relationship already established and the sincerity of your manner are all-important, not the linguistic niceties of your prayers.

In this chapter all that was intended was to give the pastor some basic content for his pastoral calls. If you are faithful to the task, you will go home some nights pretty darn tired, but you will know that you have been working at your ordination vows. And you will have left behind you some very grateful homes in your parish.

Now suppose the pastor agrees that the decline in the pastoral role is a great weakness in the contemporary church. Suppose also he has been persuaded that *the pastoral precedes the prophetic*. Is he left in the intolerable position of seeing the value of a pastoral relationship but powerless to effect it? Must he accept as a given fact of life in our time that the pastoral role is decisive, but there is simply not the time for its fulfillment? Significant help is available.

4

A PROPOSAL TO
IMPROVE BOTH PREACHING
AND PASTORAL CARE

Preaching can be greatly improved and better pastoral care can be given without any additional demand on the pastor's time. This is not a theory. It is a fact that has been demonstrated. The remainder of this book is a report on that demonstration.

Two years ago I brought together eight pastors of churches whose membership ranged from two hundred to six hundred. In each case the church was a single-pastor church. Each man had the full responsibility for all the preaching and all the pastoral care. When I made the claim that the preaching from each pulpit could be significantly improved and the pastoral duties better carried out without any additional time being spent each week, they were skeptical but definitely interested.

These men had the most backbreaking assignment possible in modern society. Only one who intimately knows the pastor's life, the work schedule, and the impossible demands made upon him can appreciate the magnitude of the task. Having served a single-pastor church for years, I knew what these men were up against. I have looked back on that task from the comparative ease of being a college president. Emil Brunner once remarked that the call to serve a parish single-handedly, and to do it well, is the heaviest load any man can carry.

After I had explained to these pastors the main outline of the program I proposed, it was agreed that I would meet with the official board of each church. These meetings brought home to me again the deep dedication and the spiritual perception of the men and women who are lay leaders. They are baffled by the problems confronting the church in our time. They are often frustrated and even angered by denominational actions. Official boards are sometimes accused of being the bottlenecks in the parish. But I was amazed at their openness to the new program I was proposing. Every one of the eight church boards I visited that summer voted to enter the program.

I always began by describing the impossible task of their pastor, as I understood it from my own experience. He is supposed to be an able administrator, a religious education specialist, and a community leader. He is expected to visit the sick, to bury the dead, and to marry the marrying. In our hectic society, his counseling load grows apace. He is to bring in new members, to revive the interest of those out at the edges, and to be a leader of youth. He is expected to read widely, to study diligently, and to be a well-informed man. He is to be on call at any hour of the day or night. Then, on Sunday mornings, about forty-eight of them in a year, he is expected to preach like Paul.

The members of each official board began to see afresh that the church expects the impossible from the pastor. Small wonder that men break under the load, or leave the ministry, or just settle for a very mediocre way of doing things, with never the fresh, vibrant, inspiring feeling of a spiritual leader who is on top of his responsibilities. Before I made my proposal for the relief of his work load, we talked at length about the rigorous nature of the task and how badly we need to move toward a situation where the pastor can more nearly feel that he is a herald of the gospel and a shepherd of souls.

I then told the official board I was convinced that the preaching could be improved and pastoral care given better attention without any additional time demands on the pastor. Like the clergy before them, they did not see how that was possible, but they were willing to be shown.

The program I proposed was quite simple. The first part called for their pastor to team for a year with another pastor serving a similar-size church. The two pastors would exchange pulpits four times a year. If the sermon took an average of ten hours weekly to prepare, here would be four weeks without sermon preparation during the year, or forty work hours saved for each pastor. Since each man would naturally choose one of his best sermons when he was exchanging pulpits, the preaching should be improved in both churches that Sunday. This became known as the "exchange" sermon in any discussion of the plan.

The second part of the program called for the pastor to repeat quite deliberately three or four of his sermons during the year. For example, having worked through the fall quarter, he would have eight or ten sermons prepared and preached. At the end of the quarter he would repeat the one he thought was his best or the one most people requested. If he placed the titles in the bulletin some Sunday, parishioners could be asked to indicate the one they had found most helpful. This would be done three or four times a year. Again, on the Sundays when he was going to repeat a sermon, the pastor would be freed from sermon preparation. If he repeated three or four sermons in the course of a year, thirty or forty man-hours would be saved for the work of the parish. This became known as the "repeat" sermon.

On the matter of repeating sermons there were some humorous expressions by members of official boards. "We just assumed that he did this but disguised them fairly well." That remark brought some laughter. The old idea that the pastor had a "barrel" which he turned upside down every so often was brought up several times.

One man said: "Our pastor preached a series of sermons on the Lord's Prayer, and I would like to hear the entire series again." I saw a light on the pastor's face as he heard this request for the repeating of an entire series he had preached.

I asked how many could name a movie they had seen more than once. Many hands went up. I asked if there was any music they enjoyed hearing more than once a year. Again there was general agreement. They began to see that when a sermon has been carefully prepared and when people have found it helpful, there is something perverse and foolish about the idea that it should never be heard again in that congregation.

In several meetings with official boards the question was raised as to whose choice it should be when a sermon was to be repeated. Should it be the pastor's decision only, or should the people have some say in the selection? We talked of using the simple device of printing the titles of the last six or eight sermons in the bulletin some Sunday, and asking the congregation to mark their choice or to speak to the pastor at the door about a sermon they would like to hear again. Someone observed that if he were going to be asked to help choose which sermon was to be repeated, he would listen to all of them just a little more carefully.

The third and last phase of the program was that the pastor would deliberately preach someone else's sermon two or three Sundays a year. This would be noted in the bulletin each time it was done, and clearly indicated from the pulpit. Here again, each Sunday when another man's sermon was preached the pastor would be relatively free from sermon preparation during the week. If this were done two or three times a year, twenty or thirty additional man-hours would be available for the work of the parish. This became known as the "borrowed" sermon.

The goal to be achieved by exchanging pulpits three or four times a year, by repeating several sermons, and by borrowing would be to free the pastor from sermon preparation ten weeks during the year. With the average time in sermon preparation being eight to ten hours, the program would release something like eighty to one hundred work hours for the concerns of the parish in the course of a year.

The preaching would be improved in each pulpit, for all three types of sermons—the exchange, the repeat, and the borrowed—would be better than the new sermon the pastor would have prepared in each of those weeks. The work of the parish would be greatly enhanced, for here would be several hours of the pastor's time released each week when he did not have the task of sermon preparation. If over the course of a year something approaching one hundred work hours were freed, the pastoral work clearly should be better.

What was the reaction from the official boards? These

laymen were far more ready for such an experiment than the pastors had expected them to be. They were concerned about the work load of their pastor. They felt that the church was losing ground in our society. Their questions were far more simply requests for clarification than in any sense doubtful that the program could be carried out. Concerning the whole program, one woman said: "The church had better do something. What have we to lose by trying it?"

One deacon suggested that there be no pulpit exchange on Sundays when Communion or Baptism was to be observed, and all readily agreed. At a Lutheran church, with its high tradition of liturgy, one layman expressed the desire for no exchange on such Sundays as All Saints', Christmas, Easter, or Pentecost. Again, this seemed to be a valid point and was readily agreed upon. One board member was concerned about pastors exchanging whose parishes overlapped, for they might be accused of sheep-stealing. We agreed that we would keep some distance between the churches that were to be paired in this way for pulpit exchange.

In addition to time being saved for the pastoral function, members of several official boards pointed out that this exchange of pulpits would be a witness to our basic Christian unity. Several also made the point that two pastors would get to know each other and share ideas about their work, in addition to simply exchanging pulpits. I had some other values in mind but wanted them to come up out of the experience of the exchange of pulpits rather than speak of them in advance.

One enthusiastic elder asked: "What possible objection could anyone have to this exchange of pulpits?" To this I replied: "Someone in your congregation is sure to say, 'We're paying Reverend Smith to preach for us, and I don't see why he should be free all week and then have someone else do the preaching for him on Sunday.'" I still think there must be one like that in every church, but we met nothing of that attitude in any official board.

These were the principal points made concerning the exchange sermon by the various official boards. They were uniformly enthusiastic about trying it. Likewise the idea of the repeat sermon was well received. It just seemed good sense that when a pastor had worked up a helpful sermon it should not be filed away forever on Monday morning. The principal discussion about the repeat sermon was simply about the process of the selection. In most instances members of the official boards thought it would be well to involve the congregation in the choice of the sermon to be used again.

It was the borrowed sermon that provoked most discussion. "Don't pastors do this now and just not tell the congregations about it?" That idea surfaced several times. My reply was that stealing is stealing, whether it's chickens or sermons. I was saying that a man should borrow from time to time, but that in every case the source should be announced from the pulpit or printed in the order of service—preferably both.

I was asked to indicate the sources of sermons available to their pastor. Since I was working with several different denominations, I would mention the names of the well-known preachers in the particular denomination to which the official board to whom I was speaking was related. In some cases there was a feeling that the pastor should borrow sermons that had been preached by leaders of their own denomination. On the other hand, quite a few laymen made the point that here was an opportunity to hear preaching outside their own tradition.

Most of these churches were involved in the Consultation on Church Union. I pointed out to each official board where this was the case that the impetus for the Consultation arose from Eugene Carson Blake's sermon entitled "A Proposal Toward the Reunion of Christ's Church," preached in Grace Cathedral in San Francisco. Regardless of what people think of church union, that sermon has been more decisive for Protestantism in America than any other preached in the last quarter century. The pope requested a copy of Blake's sermon, for he recognized how important it was going to be in the whole movement for Christian openness, if not unity. However, millions of Protestants never heard the sermon, nor even knew that it existed. There was general agreement among the official boards that it would have been helpful to have their congregations hear it, and doubly so since it would have relieved their pastor from sermon preparation that week.

With the official boards I usually referred also to Pope John XXIII and the new feeling between Protestants and Roman Catholics. This era of openness and friendliness had been welcomed by these laymen. I pointed out that Pope John XXIII's *Pacem in Terris* had been addressed to all men of goodwill and was one of the most influential messages by any Christian leader in the twentieth century. It had been widely distributed in the media, and every pastor had seen either the full text or selections from it. Again there was the feeling right through the official boards that their people should have heard *Pacem in Terris* and that during the week preceding that Sunday their pastor would have had several hours freed for pastoral concerns.

This matter of the borrowed sermon will be dealt with

in greater detail later, but it is important to note here that members of the official boards recognized the very valuable material available to their pastors. This was the area of the program in which I expected to encounter some reluctance. These are the problems of the pastor, not of the people, as we shall see. The laymen recognized that rich material is available to their congregations by having their pastor preach someone else's sermon from time to time.

That summer I met with eight official boards to explain the program of exchanging, repeating, and borrowing. The whole point was to improve the preaching and to give better pastoral care from the same number of man-hours the pastor was now expanding on these two aspects of his task. Following the discussion, and before any action was taken, I always left the meeting. The matter was to be settled between the official board and the pastor. Every one of the eight boards voted to enter the program.

How were the congregations to be informed? Of course each pastor spoke of it from the pulpit whenever he planned to exchange, or to repeat, or to borrow. But a Baptist church did something far better. A member of the official board went before the congregation one Sunday morning to explain the program. He reported about the meeting with me and the open discussion within the board of the various phases of the program. He indicated some of the questions that had been raised by his fellow board members. He then informed the congregation that the official board had voted unanimously to participate. This seemed a very wise procedure, for the decision in each case was made by the official board and the pastor together, and a report to the congregation by a layman was most desirable.

Last year when a United Church of Christ congregation came into the program the following article appeared in their church paper which goes into every home:

"Dr. Joseph E. McCabe, Coe College Chancellor, was present for our September Church Council meeting to explain a program occurring among eight churches of the area last year. All eight churches asked to participate again for the coming year, with the desire that the number in the program be expanded. Three steps are included: 1. The churches are paired off, with the pastors of each pair exchanging pulpits four times during the year, using a sermon they have already used in their own congregation. 2. Each of the participating pastors reads a sermon from a nationally known minister three times a year, telling his congregation when he is doing it. 3. Each pastor repeats one of his own best sermons three times a year.

"The ten weeks, then, when there is no sermon preparation involved, would give the pastor an approximate one hundred additional hours during the year to be used in some other way decided upon by Council and pastor together.

"Hope Church Council voted unanimously to enter the program, and to decide at a later date how the additional time is to be used." (*Hope Comes Calling*, Sept. 23, 1971, Hope United Church of Christ, Hiawatha, Iowa.)

While the lay reporter did not use exactly the language the pastor or I would have employed, still the message was clear. Every home knew that the official board and the pastor had worked this out together and that it was official church policy. As we shall see farther on, when the program was evaluated in that church a year later, it received an overwhelming endorsement from the congregation.

With that formal action of eight official boards two years ago we were launched into the program. The following chapters relate our experiences with the exchange sermon, the repeat sermon, and the borrowed sermon. But here let me recall some of the changes that have occurred.

At the close of the first year's experience, four of the original eight pastors received calls to other churches. Each of the four pastors, as he left, indicated that he wanted to find a "partner" pastor in his new location and to develop with him such a program. Naturally the timing was affected by these changes, so that the number of Sundays when a pastor was freed from sermon preparation varied among the men.

Now we are well into the third year of the program. Other churches and pastors have indicated an interest in joining the original group. In every case I have met with the official board. After we talked it through, not a single board declined the invitation to participate in the program. Clearly the laymen have come to an understanding of the magnitude of the task that the modern pastor faces. They want to get on with some way to relieve that burden. Our plan calls for better preaching and better pastoral care, within the same time schedule the pastor has been following. The denominations represented in the program are: Baptist, Christian, Lutheran, Methodist, Presbyterian, United Church of Christ.

5

THE EXCHANGE SERMON

We are out to improve the preaching in each pulpit. When a man goes to another church to exchange on any given Sunday, he quite naturally preaches one of his better sermons. That's the whole idea. If a man prepares nine or ten sermons in a quarter, he should select one of those which his own people found most helpful. Better preaching in both pulpits is obviously the result on exchange Sunday.

Better pastoral care is our second aim in the program. When the pastor goes to his study on Monday morning of the week he is to exchange, he has those precious ten hours or so which are usually devoted to sermon preparation to allocate for other pressing needs of the parish. This is all so obvious that it needs no further elaboration here. What a lift it is for the spirit when one can begin a week in which so many working hours have been freed for direct pastoral work, study, or however the pastor chooses to use the additional time. But in addition to better preaching and better pastoral care, we have discovered other benefits from the exchange program.

The burden of the Protestant church is that it is preacher-centered and therefore any particular congregation is always in danger of becoming a personality cult. The exchange program helps to drain off the idolatry of the incumbent, which is present to some degree in every parish.

Ask any Roman Catholic friend to tell you who celebrated Mass at his church last Sunday. If it is in a parish with more than one priest on the staff, the person may be unable to recall who was the celebrant. But ask any Protestant who preached at his church last Sunday and he will tell you immediately. We glory in our tradition of the pastor who is the shepherd of his flock, known and loved by his people. This is a great strength of the Protestant ministry. But have we taken seriously the spiritual problem posed for our parishioners by a tradition that has so exalted preaching that there is an excessive attachment to the pastor?

One of the more perceptive pastors in our exchange program last year wrote this: "The most important element of all about this program is the possibility it offers to help strengthen the congregation as congregation and eliminate excessive preacher-centeredness." We are hearing much these days about the renewal of the parish. Certainly this means the spiritual strengthening of individuals and a lively sense of the supporting fellowship. The same man goes on: "Further [the exchange program] has the potential of helping preachers realize, if only slightly, that the Kingdom of God does not rest squarely upon their individual shoulders."

Another important element or by-product of the exchange program is that each church has a "second pastor" to whom the people can turn in time of need if their own pastor is not available. The frantic pace of the ministry in our day takes a man out of his parish far more often than was formerly the case. The emphasis on continuing education was much needed and long neglected, but it means that a man may be out of town from ten days to two weeks sometime during the year, other than when he is on vacation. Church conferences are held at a distance from the pastor's home and he may be gone two or three days at a time more than once in a given year. Then of course there are those weeks when, he hopes, he is hundreds of miles away from his parish on vacation. To whom do his people turn for help when their pastor is away?

It seems to the congregation perfectly right and natural to turn to the pastor who has preached for them. Last year a Baptist and a Presbyterian had exchanged pulpits several times. Late in the year the former had to be out of town for several days attending a church conference. On the day he was to leave, there was a death in the congregation. He made the pastoral call and explained to the bereaved family that he had a long-standing commitment to go to this conference but would nevertheless certainly abide by their wishes in the matter. The family said they had heard the Presbyterian pastor in their own pulpit, felt they already knew him, and would be perfectly satisfied to have him conduct the services in order that their own pastor could continue with his plans to attend the conference. This was done, the Presbyterian exchange pastor conducted the funeral service, and their own pastor visited them again when he returned home. The exchange pastor had ministered to them, and "not as a stranger."

Still another valuable by-product of the exchange program is simply to have the pastor experience the welcome and acceptance of another congregation. We easily become very myopic in our vision of the task. Although he may have the very best of relationships with his own people, it is good for the pastor to stand in another pulpit, to feel the response of that congregation, and to greet those people after the service. This is not simply having the ego massaged by more and different people. It is a very legitimate and healthy need to experience Christian worship and fellowship beyond the confines of one's own parish. In notes written for me after a series of exchanges, two pastors say almost identical things. One observed: "I have been received very warmly by Olivet people and feel very much at home there." The other wrote: "The exchange was stimulating to me. I enjoyed the very warm and open reception I received at Marion Christian. . . . After the first Sunday I felt at home."

The witness to our basic unity in Christ is a value that was seen by several official boards when I visited them to discuss the program. This point keeps emerging again and again as we go along. Baptists, Presbyterians, Methodists, Lutherans, Disciples, and members of the United Church of Christ—these churches represent the broad spectrum of Protestantism in America. Discussions of church union and plans for mergers of various denominations have had periods of great acceptance in this country. Likewise there have been periods of very low interest. But the exchange program is not an argument for union or a strategy for merger. It is simply an experience of our basic oneness in Christ. A Lutheran pastor exchanged for a year with the pastor of a much less liturgical Christian church. The latter recently moved from our community. Looking back on his year's exchange, he wrote: "Working with Cedric Lofdahl of the Lutheran tradition was educational, as well as a warm and friendly experience. It was apparent that our diversity in liturgy and polity was revealed in preaching traditions, sources, and training. But I highly recommend pulpit exchanges across liturgical lines for both the preacher and the congregation."

Now let us look into the interior life of a pastor and see how the exchange program relates to his healthy self-image and self-acceptance. In scarcely any other profession, unless it be that of the politician, are comparisons between individuals so readily made, and often, just as in the case of politicians, not on the real merits of those involved. I mean simply that a pastor who is afraid of how he measures up with other men as a preacher and is defensive about his own pulpit can scarcely be enjoying good mental health. The following is quoted at some length, for it deals with the problem so clearly. It was written by one of our pastors after a year in the exchange program. He said I could make any use of his observations that might be helpful to other pastors.

"We all have a little trouble holding our image. To become big enough to praise and see others in a better light than yourself is a goal in the ministry. Ministers are almost 'showmen' though they know it is out of context in our work. But it is there.

"How could I come on as strong as my partner in preaching? Such a childish, shameful thought, but it is usually there for those of us who are honest.

"To exchange pulpits meant a good hard look at my weakness and my strength. What I have in presentation is as valid as my partner, but may not always be as acceptable to a congregation as another's work. To get beyond this problem of comparison, of course, is freedom. I had to learn once again and experience that freedom with the pulpit exchange.

"My work must be on an individual evaluation and what the Christ has given me, rather than ratings by friend or foe or group or congregation. Acceptance—self-image must grow healthy for this to happen.

"The preaching program you have adopted squeezes and crunches one into that freedom, if he will let it. At the time you called us together, I was in great need for that freedom lesson once again. I am free to do and be what I am in Christ's evaluation. How often that lesson must be learned and relearned. I think you can read between the lines."

This pastor was wrestling quite honestly with a very real spiritual problem, not at all uncommon in the ministry. It is all tied up with the fact that love of God requires a very healthy dose of self-love. But self-love and self-acceptance are not possible if we are sitting on the edge of our personalities to see how we are being compared with others. Far better to accept "what the Christ has given me" and to rejoice, whether it be one, two, or ten talents as a preacher.

In contrast to an unhealthy lack of self-acceptance, one of our pastors wrote the following in the church paper which goes into all the homes of his congregation. He and his preaching partner had exchanged several times last year and as summer approached he wrote the following for the church paper:

WHAT A DELIGHT—

. . . to hear all the good comments after each pastoral exchange Sunday. That Francis King, I'd sure like to hear him preach sometime! If you're in the same boat, you've got one more chance yet this year. So be watching for the date.

Isn't it refreshing to see a pastor writing like that about a fellow minister who comes to his pulpit from time to time? There's a man who has entered into the freedom in Christ that was described above and that is so necessary if one is to enjoy mental health and have any degree of spiritual power in his own ministry.

A further value of the exchange program must be obvious by now. The pulpit exchange helps prepare the congregation for the day when they will have a new pastor. Reference was made earlier to the preacher-centeredness of much of Protestant church life. We have all witnessed the decline in church attendance, and often in financial support, when a pastor accepts the call to another church. This happens far too often to be viewed as an isolated or a minor problem. In almost any congregation you will find people out at the edges of the church's life. Their names are on the parish registry. They may attend at Easter and at Christmas and they may give some support to the budget. But where is that fervor and enthusiasm which once they knew and which others will tell you they once showed? The truth is they are worshiping some Apollos who preached in that church a decade or more ago.

If they had heard another voice in the pulpit from time to time, and had been led in worship by someone other than their idol, they just might have gotten the big idea that the gospel would continue to be preached in that place after their bright and shining light had moved on to other pastures. Four churches where the official boards voted to join our program, and where there were pulpit exchanges, have seen their pastors accept calls in the past two years. We would like to think the exchange sermon helped them to be prepared for the day when a new pastor would come to town and begin his ministry among them.

One of the pastors wrote this evaluation of the pulpit exchange: "By far the most vital part of the program for both myself and our people. Many excellent comments— even brought back two families who have not been active because of being turned off by me. They were present for two of the three exchange Sundays." If a man has been serving a church for several years and no one is disaffected by him, he shouldn't think he is the perfect pastor and preacher. Rather, he should ask whether he has been "declaring the whole counsel of God," which was his ordination vow. Here is a parish where people who were unhappy with the incumbent did come out when another pastor was to preach.

Last summer we asked members of participating congregations to write comments about the exchange program. Here are notes by people in three different churches. "We are very prejudiced in favor of our own pastor, but if it will help Steve with his work load, we would naturally approve of the pulpit exchange." That should have set up the pastor for a week! In another church, where the pastor's first name is Peter, a parishioner wrote: "I'm pretty partial to a man called Peter's sermons." Another wrote: "Exchanging pulpits is a good idea—we need new faces occasionally and we can learn about other congregations in the city."

"Do you approve of his [the pastor's] exchanging pulpits with another pastor from time to time during the year?" That question was asked of over three hundred people in six of the participating churches following a year's experience with the pulpit-exchange program. The combined replies were 93 percent in the affirmative. When the results from one of the six churches are omitted, the response was a 98 percent approval. We consider that a working majority.

Finally, one of the values of the exchange program is the very good experience of having a fellow pastor with whom you look down the road as you plan your dates to be in each other's pulpits. If you establish an exchange relationship with a pastor with whom you are really congenial, there is a resulting friendship and a sharing which is often denied to those who serve single-pastor churches. In large churches where there is more than one pastor, the senior pastor not only has an ordained associate but often other professionally trained members of the church staff. Planning together is a natural and necessary part of the relationship. But the pastor who is the only professionally trained person serving his church lacks this experience of sharing and planning. It does not always turn out in the following manner in our program, but it can:

Lyle and Frank were teamed as preaching partners this past year. Each reported that during the year he was having good experiences in the other's pulpit. It is my practice to visit with each pastor in the program during the summer, to see how things have gone for him and to see how he feels about continuing with his exchange partner. I missed visiting Lyle this summer and so telephoned him about the first of September, thinking we should talk things through. As soon as he knew why I was calling, he said: "Frank and I have a date for coffee to go over the schedule and set our exchange Sundays." And all this time I thought I was in charge here!

We began by seeking better preaching and better pastoring through the exchange program. Both have been accomplished. But to paraphrase a New Testament passage: "All these other values have been ours as well."

6

THE REPEAT SERMON

Some pastors have an honest reticence about repeating a sermon. Their official boards and their parishioners do not share that feeling. This has come through again and again in our program. If the exchange sermon is the one with the greatest satisfaction to the pastor, it is the repeat sermon that finds greatest acceptance with the congregation.

In our home it just wouldn't be the Christmas season without the playing of Handel's *Messiah* on the stereo. Have we heard it forty times already? Far more, I'm sure. And it is loved, of course, for its soaring beauty and triumphant affirmation. But in addition, the music is appreciated simply because it is so well known, and our minds run ahead to each theme before it is really heard. Familiarity has bred appreciation. But of course it is familiarity with something superb. We should occasionally produce a sermon that makes our own spirits soar, and when we do, it should be clearly marked "to be repeated."

Nothing seems easier than for a pastor to repeat a sermon that he has preached before. Actually it is not that simple. The heart of the problem is that the pastor is afraid he will be caught repeating! There has grown up in the Protestant tradition the myth that each Sunday morning the preacher has a fresh sermon, prepared that very week, wrought out by lonely wrestling with the Scriptures—a task to which he has been solemnly ordained and "set aside from all common and ordinary uses."

It is also a very real and true assessment which sees that same preacher, when called to a new congregation, "turn the barrel upside down" and use in substance, if not in identical form, many of those sermons he preached in his last church. What is needed is the clear recognition by the pastor that his people welcome hearing again those better sermons of his which they have heard before. When he understands that, let him clearly state from the pulpit or print in the order of service, or both, that on this particular Sunday he is repeating a sermon which he has preached from that pulpit before and which people said they found helpful. That is justification enough. When he couples with that statement the explanation that he has had eight to twelve additional hours for pastoral duties that week, he is freed from the old fear of being found out, and his people know he has not used the time on the golf course or by the trout stream—at least not all of it.

"Before each sermon which was a part of the program, I gave a brief verbal statement of purpose. Consequently the congregation was always cognizant of the program and well disposed to it. It was a rewarding sidelight that people were thinking about sermons worthy of repeating before asked to do so."

The pastor in our group who wrote that was one who asked his people to help decide which sermons should be repeated. It certainly sharpens one's listening when one knows he will be asked to express an opinion about the worth of the sermon. It isn't just "better preaching" that comes through the program of the repeat sermon. Quite clearly it's "better listening" also. And what preacher wouldn't like to achieve that!

One pastor in our program who asked his people to help him choose which sermons he would repeat wrote: "The idea of their choosing my best makes them better listeners." I have not referred to the very desirable feature of giving people a sense of participating in the preaching task, which is part of their responsibility as believers. It isn't simply making them better listeners, which is good, but also helping them to see and to share the witnessing function of the church.

Here are other reactions by pastors to the program of repeating sermons. "No problem at all with this. I usually reworked them a little, which of course made them seem more fresh in delivery." Another wrote: "This has been the most convenient phase, especially for a pastor who may be using a liturgical calendar with appointed text. He merely searches his file for the appropriate date and sermon." And another: "If not done mechanically—that is, on a predetermined schedule—but rather when the subject matter seems appropriate, it has been good." Those three statements are from pastors of three different denominations. Each sermon repeated by those three pastors was very likely much better than the new one that each would have written for the week. Each sermon repeated represented eight to twelve hours saved for the work of the parish that week. In each case, after the congregation had a year's experience with the repeat sermon, the parishioners voted overwhelmingly in favor of it.

Here is the statement of another pastor concerning the repeat sermon: "Benefits—encourages participation with the minister in the preaching witness; the people have some voice and power in selecting sermons; a means of feedback to the preacher on the sermons that are well received. Difficulties—the preacher overcoming the feelings that his material is stale; the fear of boring people who are second-timers on a sermon." I think the latter fear is very real with many pastors. They simply feel that, having said a thing, they should let it go at that. But they should be aware of how very, very little of our wisdom is remembered by our people. What our receiving apparatus picks up by hearing is what is most quickly forgotten. The written word and the visual image have it all over the spoken word as far as remembering is concerned. The idea that, having once "told" our people something, we can assume they have both heard and remembered it is comforting, but it's light-years away from reality.

Early in my ministry I was discussing preaching with the very wise dean of our theological seminary. I complained that I had tried to engage someone in conversation about the sermon I had preached the previous Sunday and to my utter dismay he could not recall what my theme had been. When I had recounted the incident and how downcast I felt about it, the dean suddenly asked: "What did you have for lunch last Wednesday?" I told him I couldn't possibly remember. His quick rejoinder was: "It did you good, didn't it?" He was a wise man.

We need to understand that much of the Sunday morning worship hour is supportive therapy. It is manna for the day or for the week. If a pastor wants to be shocked into reality, let him ask a parishioner to give a brief re-cap of last Sunday's sermon. Don't let the reply floor you. It was good for that hour, and it was spiritual therapy for jaded spirits. Just recognize that our preach-ing efforts are not long remembered and that to repeat the best of them is sound teaching procedure. It is also good stewardship of the preacher's time.

How often can you repeat a sermon? "As long as you can glow over it." That's an old piece of advice which has been around for many years. I don't know who said it first, but I know it is helpful. If you have wrestled with a Biblical passage until it has come alive for you and gripped your own soul, you can be fairly certain it will grip others also. If you preach on the central tenets of the faith, not simply on the passing scene, you will produce from time to time a sermon that warms your own heart and helps you to understand this puzzling pilgrimage. That's a good sign that the sermon is worth repeating. This is especially true in pastoral preaching, where it is "the great truths which heal." Sermons on providence, prayer, and suffering are those which do not necessarily display your erudition or call for yet another analysis of some contemporary crisis. But they do their effective work in the depths of bewildered souls, and their repeti-tion only makes those sermons more helpful.

I have done my share of cosmic problem-solving in the pulpit, and from time to time have foisted on an unsus-pecting congregation my own toccata and fugue in the grand manner. But what has kept me going as a preacher has been the quiet word at the door: "I was helped this morning." Or something I have remembered and cher-ished a long time now: "That's a sermon I need to hear every now and then." Should the preacher put aside such expressions of gratitude and plunge into something new every Monday morning as long as he serves that church? This is to deny the wishes of his people and to refuse those unmet parish needs for still another week.

My own best experience with the repeat sermon is entitled "Were You There?" Peter Marshall prepared this sermon when he was at the New York Avenue Presbyterian Church in Washington, D.C., borrowing quite extensively from the book entitled *By an Unknown Disciple*. When I use the sermon, the note in the order of service is this:

Sermon Topic: "Were You There?"
               (With acknowledged indebtedness
               to Peter Marshall)

This sermon is far more effective than anything I have ever written about the crucifixion. I repeated it in two parishes I served, and have preached it once for several others. In the city where we now live I have used it three times in the same church for union Good Friday services. Just a few days ago I was asked to preach it again next Good Friday. It is an example of both the repeat sermon and the borrowed sermon. It is an effective and moving treatment of the atoning death of Christ. With that note in the order of service, I feel very good about using it and about repeating it.

One of the most moving worship services of my seminary days was when Clarence McCartney preached in the chapel on the topic "Come Before Winter." That is exactly as the words appear in Paul's second letter to Timothy. It did not detract in the least that we knew he had preached on that theme every fall for more than a dozen years for his own congregation. You might expect that many people, noting that topic for the sermon next

Sunday and having heard his sermon on that theme several times, would decide not to come to church. Just the opposite is the case. For nearly two decades McCartney preached on that theme every fall, always announcing it in advance, and the church was always full.

If any man can repeat a sermon every year for nearly a quarter of a century, should not we lesser lights repeat our best work at least once? And if you develop a sermon that seems especially helpful to your people, consider preaching it every year as long as you are serving that congregation.

Of course, there is no copyright on that passage which Paul wrote to Timothy, so, if the text grips you and fires your homiletical imagination, consider developing your own sermon on the topic "Come Before Winter." Or, take the Advent theme that though we deserve to be abandoned by God, and in our own righteousness have no claim on his mercy, still he comes again to call us back to himself. "The Soul's Second Chance" is a theme worthy of being preached the first Sunday in Advent every year. A striking text for the sermon are these words of Jesus in the parable: "Last of all, he sent unto them his son." Another time for a sermon worthy of being repeated again and again is when winter is passing and the first warm winds begin to blow. Consider giving it the title "God's Glorious Springtime."

To repeat too many sermons every year would be very poor judgment indeed. To repeat one or two, if they are centered on the soul's decisive relationship with Christ, can be both helpful to your people and memorable also when so much else has been long forgotten.

One of the men in our program recently told me his own soul was stirred, and his people were quite vocal in their praise, when he preached on the topic "When All Seems Lost." Several asked him to be sure to repeat that sermon. The familiar story of Elijah and his discouragement sets the Biblical background. Of course it describes every person's spirit at some time or other. That is exactly why the preacher received such a response. I venture the opinion that he could preach that sermon every year. For from seeing a sparser congregation, the minister would probably see the attendance increase that Sunday. Years after he has left that church there will be people who will remember with gratitude that just "when all seems lost" is precisely when the Spirit of the Lord comes in to strengthen, to encourage, and to lead one out into joyous discipleship.

Now that I am no longer in the parish ministry, my preaching is to a different congregation almost every Sunday that I am in the pulpit. There is a sermon in my file that I have used half a dozen times. It has the words of Jesus for the title: "Be Not Anxious." I can preach that one for myself at least once every year! If some congregation benefits as well, that's just fine. Here is another I have used three times with the same congregation, and with what response? I get requests to preach it again. Then here is a sermon manuscript entitled "Christ and Suffering." Every time I use it someone says it is a theme he needs to hear more often. And on that topic the preacher's file of illustrations should enable him to keep the theme fresh and helpful. Preach once a year on that subject and no one will complain that he has heard it before.

Here are the titles of sermons in a series of nine I once preached during September and October. The list of topics was printed on the first Sunday, which helped greatly to stimulate interest. People told me they were looking forward to certain themes, weeks in advance of when I planned to preach on those topics. I must say that "Christ and Sex" raised anticipations beyond what I was able to fulfill for some, but many said that the sermon had an impact. Here are the topics:

"Christ and Work." (First Sunday in September, Labor Day weekend)

"Christ and Education." (Opening of schools and colleges)

"Christ and Communism." (It simply is not 1917, and monolithic communism is a myth)

"Christ and History." (Judgments in history, and judgment at the end of history—Niebuhr)

"Christ and the Human Family." (Worldwide Communion)

"Christ and Suffering." (The second time that year!)

"Christ and Sex." (The gift of God and the purity of Christ)

"Christ and Politics." (It was an election year)

"Christ and Money." (Every Member Canvass Sunday)

It was very helpful and stimulating to give these titles out in advance. If I were doing it again, I would tell the people that I planned to ask them at the close of the series to indicate which one or two they would like to hear again. Then I would print the titles in the order of service the Sunday after the series was concluded and ask people to check two of them. The titles receiving the most votes would be repeated, either very soon or on some future Sundays, but definitely within that church year.

The repeat sermon offers the pastor the best opportu-

nity to improve his delivery. When you have the completed manuscript for next Sunday already at hand on
Monday morning, a sermon you have used before, your
preaching can grow in vocal power and general effectiveness that week. Take the manuscript into the pulpit
every morning for twenty minutes. Listen to the sound of
your own voice. Are you projecting every word to the
last pew, or are you dropping your voice toward the
end of each sentence? Do you hold your eye contact at
a particular point for several seconds, or do your eyes
flit from place to place, which comes off as flitting from
face to face on Sunday morning? Are your gestures mean-
ingfully related to the material, or do you saw the air at
random? Do you place your visual imagery just above
the heads of the congregation, which is effective, or do
you turn sideways and look at the wall, or worse yet, up
toward heaven? Do you vary the rate of speech to suit
the material, or is it all either monotonously slow or
feverishly fast? Do you pause for effectiveness and fill
the pause with poise, or does it all come off like a string
of boxcars, which says it is really all the same and all
rather unimportant?

The sad fact is that so many pastors make little prog-
ress in preaching effectiveness after leaving their voice
critic at the theological seminary. Many pastors have told
me that all the time which they can squeeze out for
sermon preparation must go on the manuscript, leaving
little or none for the preparation of the delivery. Back
in seminary it was both their manuscript *and* their delivery that were criticized. Now, somehow, they expect
the Holy Spirit to speak for them on Sunday morning. It
might be helpful if the Spirit would speak, not so much
for a man on Sunday morning but *to* him, and say: "This
week you have been lazy."

This neglect of preparing the delivery of the sermon can be excused by the pressure of parish demands. But the week when you are repeating should be the week when you summon up the ghost of your vocal critic at seminary every morning, and with the familiar manuscript in hand go into the pulpit and "hear your own voice, and watch yourself preach." The week you repeat a sermon is the week you can grow in vocal power and in the total effectiveness of your delivery.

The preacher should make it a firm rule that each Monday morning in the study he will spend at least a half hour with the sermon he preached the day before. This is the very best way for him to improve his own art of sermon craftsmanship. Where did it go well? Where did it seem weak? Which illustration seemed to make the point? Which fell flat? If a man has any sense of rapport with his congregation while preaching, he will have a lot to say to himself about that sermon on Monday morning.

The preacher should give himself a grade on the sermon on Monday morning. Let him rigorously grade his sermons on a scale from A through D. The letter grade should be written at the top of the manuscript or on the first page of preaching notes. The A's may appear very seldom indeed, but the A sermon is the one he should consider worthy of being repeated. The D's should be dispatched to the wastebasket without benefit of decent burial. Then let him wrestle with the B or C quality sermon, to determine whether it can be reworked and improved. The notes on what needs to be done with the manuscript should be made right then, not months or years later when the pastor sees it quite cold and lifeless.

His people should know that he is going to repeat from time to time, and they should be encouraged to indicate their preference as to which sermons to hear again. Then it is in honest confrontation with the sermon on Monday morning when the preacher decides whether it is worthy of being repeated in its present form, needs reworking, or should be banished forever.

Two pastors writing about our total program made the following statements of concern about the repeat sermon. The first wrote: "I just didn't feel good about this myself and so did not repeat an entire sermon. I did reuse excerpts from previous sermons, and, of course, have used quotes over many times. I feel this lends continuity to my preaching and gives me the opportunity to say the same thing in a variety of ways. But somehow repeating the entire sermon has me turned off, so figure I should leave hands off until I can feel good about doing it." There's an honest man. Yet when the members of his congregation were asked whether they would favor their pastor's repeating a sermon now and then, they voted 85 percent in the affirmative, without ever having heard him do so! What comes through here again is the willingness of the congregation, in company with the official board of the church, to have the pastor repeat sermons in order to have more time to devote to the affairs of the parish. I have gently chided that pastor along the lines that his official board and the members of his congregation are gently nudging him toward "more time for the parish during the week" without any additional hours from him.

The other pastor wrote: "I did not use the repeat sermon, possibly because I've been so conditioned to putting out a new one each week. . . . This evaluation [by his congregation] has indicated an overwhelming approval on the part of those who responded to having some repeated. On that Sunday [when the congregation was asked about repeating] several came up to me with specific requests for which ones they wanted repeated. I gained some insights here. I will begin to use repeat sermons this year." His official board had approved. Then his parishioners had voted 90 percent in favor of repeating, without ever having heard him repeat! The result: "I gained some insights here. I will begin to use repeat sermons this year."

More than three hundred people in six of our churches were asked: "Do you approve of the pastor preaching a sermon that you may have heard before?" The least percentage of approval among the six churches was 85 percent. One congregation approved by a 96 percent vote. The average for all six congregations was 90 percent in the affirmative. As has been noted, two churches voted 85 and 90 percent approval respectively, even when their pastors had not given them the experience of hearing a repeat sermon.

When the suggestion for repeating several times in the year has been honestly presented to an official board and to a congregation, for the purpose of freeing more man-hours for the work of the parish, I have never known either to vote anything but an overwhelming approval. Of course, "I've been so conditioned to putting out a new one each week" may constitute a barrier in the mind of some pastor. No barrier exists with his official board and his people.

7

THE BORROWED SERMON

If by chance a layman is reading this, he should get a
firm grip on his chair. What comes through very clearly
from the pastors is that the borrowed sermon is the most
difficult part of the program. Exchanging simply involves
mutual scheduling with the partner pastor, and we have
discussed the ways in which repeating can be made a
good experience for both pastor and people. The average
layman simply assumes that borrowing a sermon is a fre-
quent practice, and he certainly does not see it as difficult. On the other hand, and to a man, the pastors report
it to be the part of the program that should be done least
often, and they unanimously report it to be the least easy
of the three aspects to carry off well.

At the same time, one pastor gives this rather glowing
report. "Let me share from my experience with the re-
nowned sermons. I began with James Stewart's 'Why Be
a Christian' and used Martin Luther King's 'Letter from
Birmingham Jail' on Race Relations Sunday. As one not
well acquainted with the preaching of James Stewart, I

discovered a simplicity and intensity that fit my style very well. Dr. Stewart's ability to picture-frame ideas was a memorable part of the sermon. The experience was very good, and the response of the congregation was almost evangelical in enthusiasm. Several persons set out to tell others about what they had missed in worship."

I submit that if any pastor will take Stewart's sermon on that theme, "Why Be a Christian," in *The Gates of New Life* (Charles Scribner's Sons, 1938), and spend twenty minutes with it each morning of the week, he will be a better man by Sunday. Moreover, his congregation, on hearing it, will be quite vocal in their appreciation. Of course, if the pastor thinks he can produce something better than Stewart's that week, let him go on thinking that way, depriving his people of a genuine spiritual experience and leaving still unfinished good work in the parish which the eight or ten hours freed from sermon preparation could have seen accomplished.

Stewart's sermon is a magnificent affirmation of faith, makes effective use of alliteration, and can be made memorable for any gathered congregation. Here is the simple outline: "The Christian life is Happier than any other, Harder than than any other, Holier than any other, and more Hopeful than any other." The illustrations are apt and the literary allusions rich. Here is one of the major preachers of the English-speaking world who has given us a sermon of great depth and beauty. It is equally appropriate for both a wayside country chapel and a metropolitan congregation. Yet we preachers continue to deprive our people of the experience of hearing it because of our mistaken notion that to borrow is wrong, or that we can do better than Stewart! Both points are false.

We should be perfectly clear that to borrow without giving credit is a form of stealing, and simply drains off any possibility of that integrity which is the hallmark of effective preaching. Stewart, whose sermon we have been discussing, is most helpful at this point:

"It is hardly necessary to labour the point that to borrow another man's thoughts, ideas and expressions, and to present them as one's own, may be one way of reducing labour and maintaining the supply, but in God's eyes it is to be a castaway. Here is someone, let us say, who is so preoccupied throughout the week with a medley of good works, all of them doubtless legitimate and worthy in their own way, that at the week-end, finding himself sermonless and in desperate straits, he is driven to use another man's material, 'reaping where he has not sown, and gathering where he has not strawed.' Is it likely that such preaching should ring true? May not such a habit, if persisted in, neutralize and negative the grace of the preacher's ordination? Must it not imperil his spiritual vitality, and ultimately jeopardize his soul. . . . Far better the poorest and most halting discourse that is veritably a man's own than the most elaborate work of art tainted with the breath of plagiarism. But indeed it were superfluous to emphasize this further. And where is honour towards God to be looked for if not in the work of those who are His heralds?" (*Heralds of God,* p. 175; Charles Scribner's Sons, 1946.)

The second sermon that we all read, and that some men preached, was Martin Luther King's "Letter from Birmingham Jail." It simply throbs with the Old Testament cry for justice, and yet is deeply filled with non-violence, in the spirit of Gandhi. Here are brief passages:

"For years now I have heard the word 'Wait!' It rings

in the ear of every Negro with piercing familiarity. This
'Wait' has almost always meant 'Never.' As one of our
distinguished jurists once said, 'Justice too long delayed
is justice denied.' We have waited for more than 340
years for our constitutional and God-given rights. . . .

"There comes a time when the cup of endurance runs
over, and men are no longer willing to be plunged into
an abyss of . . . despair. I hope, sirs, you can understand
our legitimate and unavoidable impatience. . . .

"I have wept over the laxity of the church. But be assured that my tears have been tears of love. There can
be no deep disappointment where there is not deep love.
Yes, I love the church. How could it be otherwise? I am
in the rather unique position of being the son, the grand-
son, and the great-grandson of preachers. Yes, I see the
church as the body of Christ. But, oh! How we have
blemished and scarred that body through social neglect
and through fear of being nonconformists. . . .

"If I have said anything in this letter that overstates
the truth and indicates an unreasonable impatience, I
beg you to forgive me. If I have said anything that under-
states the truth and indicates my having a patience that
allows me to settle for anything less than brotherhood,
I beg God to forgive me. . . .

"Let us all hope that the dark clouds of racial prejudice
will soon pass away and the deep fog of misunderstanding will be lifted from our fear-drenched communities,
and in some not too distant tomorrow the radiant stars
of love and brotherhood will shine over our great nation
with all their scintillating beauty."

One of our pastors preached it for his people and wrote
of the experience: "The Use of Martin Luther King's
'Letter' was unnerving, to say the least. I must admit my

anxieties were high before delivering this prophetic in-
dictment of white racism. But I felt it was important for
my congregation to hear Dr. King, and I knew full well
that I could not say the things Dr. King said. So in the
setting of the stage, I asked my people to listen to Dr.
King as I attempted to fill his shoes. I experienced a
satisfaction in preaching this sermon as a stand-in for a
prophet."

Let the noninvolved pastor preach King, and let the
social activist pastor preach Stewart. Each man will
grow spiritually and in preaching power. Moreover, each
congregation will be hearing preaching that is balanced,
just because it is Biblical.

One Christmas Eve I attended services in a Presbyterian church where the pastor had the reputation of
being a scholar-minister. His earned doctorate and his
long pastorates in Presbyterian churches made him a
solid figure in that denomination. Imagine my great sur-
prise to note in the order of service that the sermon
would be "Luther's Nativity Sermon." It was not just read,
but really preached with feeling and understanding. It
is so very appropriate for the Advent season, and especially fitting for the Christmas Eve service, which has
become almost a stated service in most Protestant
churches. But how many Lutherans have ever heard this
sermon, which came as a real blessing to the Presbyterians that night? There must be hundreds of Lutheran
pastors who have spent a good part of the day before
Christmas laboriously preparing their homily for the
Christmas Eve service, carefully insulating their people
from Luther's nativity sermon.

It is well within the mark to say that during the entire
decade of the sixties the religious writing that made the

greatest impact was Pope John XXIII's *Pacem in Terris*. Both the religious and the secular press quoted extended passages. From village weeklies to *The New York Times*, and from missionary sheets to the *London Economist*, the pope's material was referred to and often cited at length. *The Saturday Review* (Feb. 13, 1965) commented:

"In no religious document of our times is there a more profound awareness that peace is the one over-riding issue and challenge of our age than in 'Pacem in Terris'. . . . The central historic significance . . . may lie in the fact that the spirit of ecumenicalism went beyond the need to attain Christian unity to the need to safeguard and ennoble human destiny." And again in the same issue: "A Protestant's first reaction must be one of gratitude that the encyclical is addressed to him. . . . For the first time in Roman Catholic history he addressed a papal letter not only to his own flock but also to . . . 'All Men of Good Will.'"

Statesmen, scientists, and religious leaders came together in a week-long conference in New York to discuss the document and the implications for humanity of what the pope had set forth. One reporter wrote: "It is the first time that a large group of leaders of all religions and no religion have come together to discuss a papal letter. For it was Pope John's great encyclical, 'Pacem in Terris,' which was the starting point of the discussions."

It is safe to say that in not one Protestant church in ten was any reference made to *Pacem in Terris*. If the pastor had clipped the article out when it appeared in his denominational journal or in the secular press and had read portions of it every morning in his study for a week, his own horizons would have been expanded. Then, on

Sunday morning, he could have shared it with his congregation for their edification. He would have saved several hours for pastoral work that week, and he would not have deprived his people of acquaintance with the most significant religious writing of the decade, perhaps of the century.

Riverside Church in New York City may be the best-known preaching post in America. The sermon preached there on June 4, 1972, by Dr. Eugene E. Laubach was entitled "Hitch Your Wagon to a Star." This footnote appeared: "I am indebted for the title and insight which form the basis of this sermon to Dr. Raymond E. Balcomb." If a preacher at Riverside Church can borrow and freely acknowledge his indebtedness, is it too much to expect that the preacher in a less nationally known parish, with all the pressures of pastoral work upon him, could do the same from time to time?

A recent issue of *A.D.*, the journal of The United Presbyterian Church U.S.A. and the United Church of Christ, carried the full text of Paul Tillich's sermon "You Are Accepted." It went into well over a million homes. The editors obviously decided that this sermon in print could be helpful to the readers. It could have been very helpful also to a pastor hard-pressed to keep his own devotional life fresh. Suppose he had read that sermon through every morning of the week. When Sunday morning arrived, he could have preached it almost without notes. His own soul would have been fed every morning, and that sermon, when preached for his people, would have been better for them than his own homily for that week. Better preaching and better pastoring would have been very much the result.

I recently spoke at a meeting of pastors, all of whom

had received that copy of Tillich's sermon. Not one of those of whom I made inquiry had preached it or planned to do so. In fact, the idea had not occurred to them at all.

It is the borrowed sermon that can help the pastor give full range to the Christian view of "nature, man, and God." It is simply a fact that preachers tend to overstress those facets of the faith which are more congenial to their own thinking and experience. Vast areas of Christian faith and social insight are seldom if ever treated in their pulpits. It is quite natural that this should be the case. But the neglect of truth which might be very helpful to his parishioners is not necessary. The preacher should read other men's homiletical work, and when he recognizes some theme that grips him and that he would not ordinarily have developed himself, he should mark it for possible future use at sermon time. It would expand his own intellectual vistas, edify his people, and save precious hours some week for the parish work.

Likewise the borrowed sermon can be the basis for improving the preacher's writing style. Every man falls into definite and set ways of saying things. He tends to employ the same figures of speech, and his transitions become quite uniform. No matter how apt and fresh may be the big ideas developed, the style Sunday after Sunday remains very much the same. This dulls interest. It is like a department store that has fresh and current styles for sale in all departments but never changes the exhibits in the windows.

In theological seminary it was part of the course in homiletics to examine rigorously a variety of sermons, not simply for their historical relevance but to see in how many different forms the gospel can be cast. It was a good introduction to the wide range of homiletical style. Phillips Brooks observed that the gospel is God's gift to the imagination. Why do preachers neglect this discipline when seminary days are behind them? To continue this study of other men's sermons is to keep the mind alive. To select two or three during the course of a year and read them daily in the week they are to be preached is to work toward variety of form and expression in sermonic style. The preacher may be very diligent in choosing from the "manifold riches of the Scriptures," but if his packaging is always the same, the effectiveness is greatly lessened. Borrow discreetly, and say so. You will not only save hours for the work of the parish but your writing style will also keep that freshness which adds so greatly to the effectiveness of preaching.

When you have found, in some book or periodical, a sermon that cries out to be preached, how proceed? The poorest thing you can do is to simply carry the book or magazine into the pulpit next Sunday and read the manuscript. If it is to become your sermon, which is essential, a more thoughtful approach is called for. On Monday morning, type out the manuscript, just as you type your own sermons for best results. In every congregation there is someone who would do this typing for you. Then each morning of the week spend twenty or thirty minutes with it, pen in hand. Underline the big ideas as they are introduced. Mark the key thought in each paragraph as it appears. This is just the way a good craftsman handles his own manuscript after it has been written. On Friday morning, take the marked manuscript into the pulpit, picture the congregation there before you, and deliver the sermon. Read it through again at home on Saturday evening.

When you preach it on Sunday morning it will indeed be your sermon, for you will have done the necessary work to make it your own. The note in the order of service giving full credit to the original author will free you from the charge of plagiarism, and when you inform the congregation that you have been freed for several additional hours of pastoral work that week, they will be doubly grateful. They will recognize good preaching, and they will be glad you have been free to spend more time than usual that week with pastoral concerns.

Do we secretly think that the sound of our own voices saying our own words is the only way the gospel can be communicated to our people? That is spiritual pride doing its worst. Of course, if people think the time saved is to be spent golfing, or fishing, or just goofing off, they have every right to insist that we keep grinding out that weekly homily. But what if the pastor said to his people: "I plan to borrow another preacher's sermon twice this year. That will do two things. It will enable you to hear some of the greatest preaching in our denomination. And secondly, in each of these two weeks I will be freed to make a dozen home calls, or to read a good book on Christian education, or to visit half the shut-ins."

One of the most insightful anecdotes concerning the unacknowledged borrowed sermon is related by W. E. Sangster, the distinguished Methodist pastor in London. One summer Sunday he was in the remote hinterland with his family on their holiday, and Sangster went to the Methodist church in the village with his young son. Sangster's sermons have been printed in the religious press in Great Britain for years, and his several books on preaching have been helpful to pastors on both sides of the Atlantic. On this particular Sunday, the village pastor gave out as his sermon topic one of Sangster's themes and then proceeded to preach it, word for word, without the slightest acknowledgment of its true source. Sangster's son recognized the sermon as one he had heard in their home church. As they came out of the service the lad said to his father: "Now I know where you got that sermon, Dad."

During the past year all pastors in our program regularly received copies of Ernest Campbell's *Riverside Sermons*. They were intended for possible borrowing, or just for priming the pump, as Campbell's distinguished predecessor, Harry Emerson Fosdick, once remarked he needed other men's sermons to do for him. Stephen Root, who serves a Methodist church in our group, exchanges with Peter Morgan, the pastor of a Christian church. Shortly before they were to exchange pulpits, Steve phoned Pete to say: "I just thought I should advise you not to use Campbell's sermon "A Good Word for Piety" when you come over here next Sunday. I'm borrowing it myself this week." It turned out that Pete had indeed borrowed that same sermon and had used it in his own pulpit, so the advice was timely. Here were two men in our group, both of whom had recognized the quality of that sermon and both reported that their congregations found it helpful.

We have considered the variety of sermons available to the preacher, and to neglect this variety, at least in reading, is to condemn oneself to the danger of sameness in both style and content. However, if a preacher is to borrow twice a year over any period of time in the same parish, he will be well advised to select at least one of the borrowed sermons every year from the same preacher. When Professor Osgood was teaching at Princeton he advised his students: "Find your own poet, and settle down with him for life." That is good advice for preachers also. Most of us who sat at the feet of James Stewart in Edinburgh could preach a selection from his sermons year after year. In fact, several of us complain that our chief difficulty is to be original on any theme which Stewart has treated and which we have read or on which we have heard him preach. Fosdick of Riverside Church once had the same effect on generations of students at Union Seminary in New York.

Let each pastor "find his own preacher, and settle down with him." By that I mean, read his sermonic output and diligently study it for both content and style. Then once a year you can preach his material with grace and conviction if you acknowledge him to be the source. I have mentioned Stewart and Fosdick. Many Methodists would find great help in Sockman or Sangster. In the South, Carlyle Marney is a shining light. Ernest Campbell of Riverside Church in New York and Bryant Kirkland of Fifth Avenue Presbyterian Church there are both careful workmen. Clovis Chappel and Leslie Weatherhead have been "preachers' preachers" in our time. Choose your own man and live with him, and you will have not only a valuable source of sermonic material and a helpful critic of your own ministry but a collaborator and a spiritual companion in the homiletical task.

With this quality of material available and with preachers from the widest theological spectrum in print, the pastor has a wealth of material with which to work. Yet, as noted earlier, the borrowed sermon is the least easy of the three emphases in our program. One pastor wrote concerning the borrowed sermon: "Didn't do this. . . . Didn't really work at it enough, I suppose, but

couldn't find anything that I really felt comfortable with."
What does it say to him that his people voted 100 percent
in favor of his borrowing!

Another pastor who was in the program this year reported an excellent experience with both the repeat sermon and the exchange sermon. Concerning the repeat
sermon, he wrote: "Well received." Concerning the exchange, he was "Very well satisfied." But he did not
preach a borrowed sermon all year. When the evaluation
was done in his church, his people voted 98 percent in
favor of his borrowing. He wrote on his own evaluation
form: "Will try this . . . for the first time." Again, here
is a pastor with reticence, obviously out of concern for
the reaction of his people, although they are decisively
in favor of his doing the very thing that gave him pause.

Why is the borrowed sermon more difficult than the
repeat or the exchange sermon? I think it is an excellent
tribute to the integrity of our preachers that they find it
so. They have been doing their own work, which is good.
But it does reveal that after seminary days they have not
opened themselves to the minds and styles of expression
of other preachers. This is an opportunity for growth in
preaching power which they have been neglecting. But
deeper than that, there is just the honest recognition that
they have known borrowing to be done in a form which
is simply stealing, politely called plagiarism. How refreshing then to note one pastor's response to the part of our
program that calls for borrowing and frankly saying so.
He writes: "You don't have to feel guilty for sharing
some excellent material of another person." That lays bare
the root of the difficulty, and points the way to freedom
and power in the use of another man's sermon when it
is frankly acknowledged and appreciated.

Here are six sermons and essays of immense power and beauty. When they are read in cold print they simply cry out to be preached:

On Faith and Doubt—"Christian Certainty"

by David E. Roberts
The Grandeur and Misery of Man, p. 58
Oxford University Press, 1955

On Healing—"On Healing"

by Paul Tillich
The New Being, p. 34
Charles Scribner's Sons, 1955

On World Peace—*Pacem in Terris*, April 11, 1963

by Pope John XXIII
Published by Paulist/Newman Press

On Christian Unity—"A Proposal Toward the Reunion of Christ's Church"

by Eugene Carson Blake
The Christian Century, Dec. 21, 1960,
pp. 1508–1511

On Social Justice—"Letter from Birmingham Jail"

by Martin Luther King
The Christian Century, June 12, 1963, p. 767

On Receiving Christ—"O Come, O Come, Emmanuel"

by James Stewart
The Gates of New Life, p. 190
Charles Scribner's Sons, 1938

Suppose a pastor were to plan to borrow twice a year. The above titles give him materials for three years. Living with each sermon for a week would strengthen his own grasp of the faith and deepen his spiritual life. That would be clear gain. In addition, his people would be vastly helped, and there would be a few extra precious hours for concerns of the parish. But the devilish myth will continue to have its power and will keep these treasures from many congregations.

I have before me now those several hundred evaluations of the program, completed by members of six churches in our program. In some of the churches, as we have noted, the pastor borrowed sermons during the year, while in others the pastor did not. The least favorable vote in any of the six churches was a solid 90 percent in favor of the pastor's borrowing a sermon from time to time. In one congregation the vote was 100 percent in the affirmative. The average for all six congregations was an impressive 95 percent in favor of the pastor borrowing.

The myth in the pew is that preachers already borrow freely, which they do not. The myth in the study is that preachers should not borrow at all, which they should. The golden rule: Do it sparingly, and be sure your people know it.

8

THE PROOF

OF THE PROGRAM

The biography of Ernest Fremont Tittle, perhaps the leading study of a distinguished preacher in recent years, points to the burden of the pastorate and the centrality of preaching in the Protestant tradition. Speaking to a woman whose son was considering the ministry, Tittle said: "I have never regretted my own choice. It has been a hard life but for me an endlessly interesting one. . . . In order to do anything worth while in the Protestant ministry you must be an unusually able preacher, for Protestantism, as you know, is built around a pulpit, not an altar. And if the pulpit has nothing to say, Protestantism is doomed to die." (Robert M. Miller, *How Shall They Hear Without a Preacher?* p. 164; The University of North Carolina Press, 1971.)

We may wish it were otherwise, but Tittle's reference to the demanding life of the pastorate and the crucial role of preaching is an accurate assessment. This book is a plea for better preaching and more effective pastoral work, within the same number of hours presently devoted to both functions.

The first objective of our program is better preaching. Has that objective been attained? Reference has been made to the more than three hundred evaluation sheets completed by members of six churches in the group. The question that was asked was worded as follows: "Do you believe the preaching has been better this past year with the above program?" Any affirmative response by 50 percent would mean a very favorable judgment by the parishioners. If 65 to 70 percent would say it had been better, that would be a most significant mark indeed. The response of the people was a towering 89 percent saying the preaching had been better.

At the church where the people voted least favorably on that issue, 80 percent said the preaching had been better. In one church, 100 percent voted that the preaching had been better. I do not think the significance of that affirmation has yet fully sunk into us. We thought at the outset that we had a program in which the preaching would be improved. Certainly in our wildest hopes we never expected anything like an 89 percent vote saying that was the case.

Isn't better preaching for his people a legitimate aspiration of every pastor? Here is a program that nine out of ten parishioners say has improved the preaching in their churches. And the solid fact is that it has been attained with far less of the pastor's time being spent in homiletical preparation.

The same question was asked of the pastors of these same six churches where the parishioners responded so affirmatively that the preaching had been better this past year. It was asked of the pastors this way: "Considering all three emphases—repeating, borrowing, exchanging—do you think the preaching from your pulpit has been better because of the program?" To a man, the pastors answered "yes" to that question. I could not resist reminding some of them that at the outset they had been indeed interested but definitely doubtful that the preaching could be improved, even though fewer hours were spent in sermon preparation. Their official boards had said in effect: "Go ahead and try it." Then the experience with the program has made believers out of the skeptics.

Our second objective has been better pastoral care. Suppose during the week when he planned to repeat a sermon, the pastor spent two hours with the manuscript in ways suggested in Chapter 6, rather than the eight to ten hours usually spent in sermon preparation. If indeed he devoted to the pastoral task a part of the time that was saved, there must have been a feeling of being more on top of his role as pastor. During the week when he was going to exchange pulpits, not more than an hour or so at most would be spent on the sermon, and again several hours would be freed for other work. We saw clearly that the borrowed sermon does take more time, perhaps up to half the regular preparation time. But it does free several hours that week for the pastoral task.

The six pastors in whose churches the evaluation was done by the parishioners were asked to rank the use of the time that had been freed from sermon preparation. They indicated three separate emphases, and in this order: first, pastoral care; second, administration; and third, study. This is just to point out the obvious, namely, that time had been freed from the homiletical task, and the first use of this extra time was spent fulfilling the pastoral office.

One pastor wrote: "I do tell the people what I've done with my time when sermons have been repeated or when there is an exchange." Another pastor wrote: "The first half of the year many hours were freed to spend directing a statewide seminar on evangelism. I was free to visualize, lead planning committees, brief resource persons, publicize, and arrange the details of the seminar." Would not his people have liked to know that?

Likewise it would have been good for the congregation to hear what one pastor wrote in his evaluation: "I have used the exchange program on those weekends when I had responsibilities (heavy) elsewhere, such as: just returning from a multiday regional church meeting some distance away; church camp director, training of counselors and opening weekend of camp; and a weekend when I had a retreat for a large youth confirmation class. In each case the exchange was a 'lifesaver' and relieved me of some of the pressure on those important weekends."

One practical Lutheran layman wrote on his evaluation sheet: "If this frees the pastor for other work, I believe [the program] helpful. To expect different we need more paid help and we aren't willing to pay for that."

A Presbyterian elder phoned to report his opinion after his church had a year's participation in the program. He had been a member of the official board to whom the original presentation had been made. He simply wanted to report that they had a very good experience at their church and that he was grateful they had been invited. It is this type of unsolicited positive response that lends authenticity to our own feelings about the program.

Here is an announcement from a parish paper where the church had been participating one full year. "The Council voted unanimously at its September 13 meeting to participate again in the Better Preaching/Better Pastoring program. . . . They voted also that they wanted to exchange with the same church, Olivet Presbyterian. So the pastors have met, and have scheduled Sunday, October 18, for the first exchange. Frank King, Olivet's illustrative preacher, will lead the worship at Hope Church, Lyle will be at Olivet." (*Hope Comes Calling*, Sept. 20, 1972, Hope United Church of Christ, Hiawatha, Iowa.)

One pastor reproduced the results of the evaluation done by his parishioners and mailed them to every family in the parish. This is of course an excellent way to get reinforcement for any program, but he didn't really need it. The preaching was declared to be better in the past year by 80 percent of his people. Ninety-eight percent said that if the pastor and the official board thought it best to continue the program, they would approve. When we ask parishioners to express their opinion on some proposed course of action, a report should be given to them. In this case the very small minority of 2 percent would see clearly that the pastor and the official board were following a program that had the backing of almost the entire church family.

The eight pastors in our group last year were asked: "Have you encountered any significant objection to the program?" Seven replied "no," and the eighth wrote: "Intellectually, no—emotionally, yes." I'm sure there is still some residual feeling in at least one back pew which runs like this: "We're paying him to do the preaching for us, and why should he be free from work that week?" The very small minority holding such an opinion were negated by the response described below.

The parishioners of the six churches where the evaluation was conducted were asked: "If the pastor and your church's official board think it best to continue the pro-

gram, would you approve?" That was the most significant question in the evaluation, for it was intended to get
a response concerning the total program. In the six
churches, where more than three hundred people responded to the question, the vote was 97 percent "yes"
and 3 percent "no." In two churches the vote was 100
percent in favor. I didn't know Protestants ever voted
100 percent in favor of anything! I think that response,
more than any other single experience, confirmed to the
pastors that the program has widespread acceptance with
their people.

How can a pastor get this program started in his
church? First, he should seek out another pastor and
share the big idea with him. Almost every pastor knows
a man within easy driving distance whom he would be
happy to have as his "preaching partner." Then the pastor
should talk the idea through with one of his leading laymen and ascertain his willingness to share the presentation at the meeting of the official board. At the board
meeting it is essential that the pastor speak freely and
explicitly of the use he would make of the extra hours
during those weeks when he would be relatively free
from sermon preparation. This is the heart of the matter
for winning acceptance of the program with the official
board. After the board has approved the program, a layman should be asked to explain it to the congregation at
worship some Sunday. If there is a church paper, an article should appear there, giving the outline of the program and reporting the official action of the board. On
those Sundays when there is an exchange sermon, or a
repeat sermon, or a borrowed sermon, the pastor should
take those occasions to make reference to the entire program and give some report, as appropriate, on how he

used the time freed from sermon preparation that week.

The clue to the acceptance of the program at the outset is to have the official board understand the crushing work load of the pastor. The latter should be quite explicit as to what areas of his responsibility need more man-hours. For one pastor it is counseling; for another, study; while another may be far behind in his reading program or in his calling. Pastors may have some hesitancy about this program because of how we have historically viewed the preaching task. We have seen that the official boards and the congregations are far more understanding in this matter than the pastor thinks, once they fully grasp the demands made upon him. After a year in which his church had participated, one layman wrote: "If this lightens the load in any way for a pastor, keep it up."

Our aim in the program, and the schedule that is set forth later in the chapter, is based on the goal of ten Sundays during the year when the pastor is largely freed from sermon preparation. We had the benefit of having eight participating churches and the willingness of all their official boards before we began.

But suppose there is no such group formed or no leader to bring a group of pastors together. If one pastor has ascertained the willingness of a preaching partner, and those two churches are the only ones in the area to be involved at the outset, it may be very wise to begin with just half the number of Sundays we have been taking as an ultimate goal. Perhaps two exchanges in a year, two repeat sermons, and one borrowed sermon would be the better plan with which to begin. At the end of the year, the pastor, the official board, and the congregation could assess the situation. If the response is anywhere near as affirmative as we received, then additional Sundays could be incorporated the following year. What is needed is for a pastor to make the start, to report to his people his use of the time freed from sermon preparation, and to give the congregation the experience of "better preaching and better pastoring."

What might a schedule for the year look like, assuming the pastor is to be significantly freed from sermon preparation ten weeks of the year? If he is to work out a ten-Sunday program, our experience suggests that there be four exchange sermons, four repeat sermons, and two borrowed sermons. Any schedule should of course be flexible and subject to change. In that respect it is like the weekly work schedule. My quarrel is with the pastor who has no daily or weekly work schedule, much less a long-range preaching schedule. Of course it is the discipline of the schedule which produces freedom. A ten-Sunday schedule might look like this:

Fourth Sunday in September—The first pulpit exchange.

The church year is well started by this time.

Fourth Sunday in October—The first borrowed sermon.

If the pastor identified the sermon during his summer reading, it is "his" already.

Fourth Sunday in November—The first repeat sermon.

Let the congregation choose from among the eight or ten preached since Labor Day.

Second Sunday in December—The second pulpit exchange.

The pastor will be in his own pulpit for the first Sunday in Advent and all the remaining Sundays through Christmas and the beginning of the New Year.

Third Sunday in January—The third pulpit exchange.

Third Sunday in February—The second repeat sermon.
This time it might be the pastor's choice.

Second Sunday in Lent—The second borrowed sermon.
The aim is to have the pastor in his own pulpit throughout Lent.

The Sunday after Easter—The third pulpit exchange.
Liturgical churches call this Low Sunday. Let the pastor take one of his better sermons and redeem the times.

Second Sunday in June—The fourth pulpit exchange.

Last Sunday before vacation—The fourth repeat sermon.
This is another good opportunity for the congregation to choose from among half a dozen or so titles of sermons preached since Easter.

If the pastor has before him in his study a chart showing every Sunday in the year from September until his vacation the following summer, these ten Sundays will deserve to be circled in blue. That is the color for quality, and he can be sure that on those ten Sundays the preaching in his pulpit is going to be better than average.

At the conclusion of this past year the eight pastors were asked: "If you were to be called to another church, would you wish to take the initiative in setting up such a program with another pastor?" All eight replied that once they were established in the new parish they would want to find a preaching partner in another church and get the program under way. One pastor, in reply to that question, wrote: "By all means!"

Another pastor, who was in the program the first year and then was called to a church in another section of the country, wrote back: "One of the derivative values of the program has been better listening by my parishioners. The preaching this year has been better, and the people know it. . . . In conclusion, I would say that the program was innovative and fresh. Although I have repeated a few sermons, I have not involved the congregation in the choice. While I have borrowed ideas and passages from authors, I have seldom preached another man's sermon. Even the pulpit exchange for three times with the same church was innovative for me. Thus I feel that this program has been quite creative. I am hopeful of continuing the pulpit program in my new location, for I think it has a lot to offer my congregation and me."

While working with budding preachers in theological seminary, I always urged them to give diligent attention to their craftsmanship in sermon preparation. They should stint no time or labor and should make their wrestling with the Scriptures the prime concern of their study hours. The sermon should be their own work, without the faintest taint of plagiarism. I still believe all this implicitly. Without that disciplined commitment, no man will be offering to Christ and his congregation the best of his gifts.

In the light of our experience in these eight churches it is evident that most ministers prepare too many sermons every year. They think they are being good stewards of the mysteries of Christ. Actually it is evidence of the demonic, for it prevents better preaching and better pastoring.

"Do you wish to continue in the program another year?" When that question was asked of one pastor in our program, he simply wrote: "A must!"

9

"...AND THESE TWO
SHALL BECOME ONE"

The pastoral and the preaching are but two different forms of witness to the same gospel. The early chapters of this book dealt with the crucial nature of the pastoral role, together with some resources for accomplishing the task. The later chapters have set forth a program that both improves the preaching and releases time for the pastoral.

The prefatory word was that of Paul: "It pleased God by the foolishness of preaching to save them that believe." Unless that truth grips a man, he should stay several country miles away from any calling to the ordained ministry. Paul speaks of "the foolishness *of* preaching." There is certainly a foolishness *about* preaching, as we have seen in our program, that makes it a robber of many valuable hours of the preacher's time, far beyond what is good and proper and necessary.

Pastoral calling needs to become more prophetic, as has been maintained, in order to rescue this part of the pastor's task from the trivia of an earlier day. Preaching needs to become more pastoral in order to equip the saints with spiritual resources if they are to take up the prophetic tasks of our day. The preacher as prophet finds texts and programs almost thrust upon him in abundance —it is the theological atmosphere of our day. On the other hand, pastoral preaching has been eclipsed, and that decline, like the decline in pastoral calling, has left people ill equipped for the strains of modern life or for the demands of discipleship.

To suggest preaching themes to the prophet in our day is like offering a glass of water to a man who is going under for the third time. The latest circular from the denomination's headquarters is probably heavily weighted with the school integration issue, with our obligations to the emerging nations, and with a call to support congressional reform. These are solidly in the prophetic tradition and are crying needs in our world. To avoid them is a modern betrayal.

But what about pastoral preaching? In the "age of anxiety," instead of the gospel's succor and therapy we have been offering first a call to social action. Action springs from a sense of adequate resources. When people feel that they are sustained and empowered by a decisive relationship with Christ they are far more likely to accept the responsibilities of discipleship. It is not wise to think that people will take up causes in the name of the church if the spiritual resources are simply assumed but never made available. Some pastors would be terribly embarrassed if they were forced to preach on the text: "Come unto me, all ye that labor and are heavy laden, and I will give you rest." It just isn't their bag, they say. But those were the words of One who said of himself: "I am the good shepherd."

Pastoral preaching is Biblical preaching and is the other half of the balance. It is more akin to the supply line than to the first-aid station. It is an axiom of the military that to fight well, the troops must eat well. Have we been asking our people to fight the good fight of faith on spiritual starvation rations?

Pastoral preaching brings in wounded spirits for counseling and strengthening. Harry Emerson Fosdick once preached a sermon on the radio which was heard by a black man in deep trouble. He said to himself: "That man could help me." He went to New York and secured an appointment with the preacher. As he came out of the study following his hour with Fosdick, he said softly to the secretary: "He put all the stars back into my sky."

Pews are filled today with problem-haunted people. Does your preaching ever lead a heavily burdened soul to say: "That man could help me"? If so, thank God. If not, why not? It is pastoral preaching which enables a person to see that help is available. When he has received that help he may then help the prophet with his task. "That man could help me." When someone says that to himself, he is not responding to a call to social action or to a summons to practice stewardship. He is responding as a hurt soul to a pastoral concern that comes through from a preacher who can point the way to restoration of spirit and a glad beginning again.

Pastoral preaching should be therapy in itself. But since "every contact is a pastoral contact," every hearer is moving toward or moving away from the pastor. When it leads to counseling which issues from a spiritually healthy person, it can lead into life equipped and newly dedicated to the prophetic task of the church in our time.

The plea here is for preaching that is Biblical and

therefore balanced. The prophetic has been perceived and proclaimed. Long may it wave. May we never return to the pietistic which was divorced from reality, or to that cultural captivity in which the good news of the gospel was identified with the good life in America.

The Biblical and balanced approach now calls for faithful attention to pastoral preaching. For a generation of social activists, that will be hard to hear. As the seminary president said: "They want to go out and give people the word." But when your word has returned unto you void, then let a man honestly examine his preaching to see if it has been a faithful setting forth of the manifold riches of the gospel. A dispirited pastor might find a new depth to his ministry if he would use all the sermon preparation time for next Sunday writing out just what it means to him to hear Jesus say: "Abide in me, and I in you. . . . He who abides in me, and I in him, he it is that bears much fruit" (John 15:4, 5).

And what shall we say of that congregation which has had race but not rest, peace claims but not the peace of God, marches but no manna from heaven, and, Sunday after Sunday, prodding without providence. Some devoted Christians are simply starved for the Biblical material on prayer, suffering, and resurrection. Christ gave his disciples the clearest commandments to change the world. But he never asked them to attempt it in their own strength; nor does he ask them now.

The great majority of the Protestant clergy will continue to serve the single-pastor church, with no professionally trained staff to help. Some of us who have served the multistaffed church would say: "Don't think it's all that good with us." Specialization is good, and in large churches tasks must be shared, but there is no substitute for immersion in the total life of the parish. Out of the pastoral comes effective preaching, and Biblical preaching is the finest of pastoral care.

Recently I talked with two pastors who have been called to churches that usually have a second ordained man on the staff. Each man says he wants to "go it alone" for a while, and to delay filling the other staff position. Each reports that he is being drained, but also that he is having an experience in depth which will not be possible later. The single-pastor church may have a parallel in the field of medicine. The general practitioner is the man of whom medicine stands most in need just now. And it is significant that at the school of medicine at the university, the dean reports that more young men have indicated their preference for general practice than has been the case for many years. With due appreciation for specialization, one to one is still good medicine, and good witnessing.

There is an Old Testament verse that runs like this: "Help us, O Lord our God; for we rest on thee, and in thy name we go against this multitude" (II Chron. 14:11). The tragedy is that so many have been urged to go against the multitude of social evils in our day, without being offered that refreshment of spirit. But when the witness is Biblical, it will be balanced.

Concerning preaching and pastoral witness, surely the last word is a paraphrase of the marriage service: "What God hath joined together, let no man put asunder." Someone, grasping that central truth for his ministry, may begin again with a fresh spirit, in devotion to the One who called him, and will pledge himself to continue: "As long as we both shall live." Since that is eternity, it will take all that time to express our gratitude.